ALIEN CONSTRUCT
Extraterrestrial Biological Computers

ADULT COLORING BOOK
& CRYPTOGRAM PUZZLE

Original Artwork by C. Lee Austin

ALIEN CONSTRUCT
EXTRATERRESTRIAL BIOLOGICAL COMPUTERS
ADULT COLORING BOOK & CRYPTOGRAM PUZZLE

ISBN: 978-0-69299-584-6

FIRST EDITION: DECEMBER 2017

WWW.ALIENCONSTRUCT.COM

Don't Panic

"I stood helpless before an alien world; everything in it seemed difficult and incomprehensible." - Carl Jung, The Red Book

Carl Jung was the first psychologist to use coloring as a relaxation technique. Coloring taps into the psyche and activates different areas of our brain. The action of choosing colors and deciding where to put them involves both logic and creativity. This focus promotes a de-stressing effect.

The inspiration for these designs came to me one night in a dream - I know, creepy right? Ever since then I've felt compelled to create and share these strange, alien-like images. If you love abstract, technology-inspired art then this book will definitely interest you.

In addition to being used for coloring, this book also offers the challenge of decoding a computer-like language which is found on each of the art pages. Once decoded these simple cryptogram puzzles will spell out the name of that particular Alien Construct.

Now go grab your art supplies, it's time to be creative!

- C. Lee Austin, Artist

What is an Alien Construct?

ΛLIEN

noun: /ey-lee-uhn/

Λny life-form or object being of extraterrestrial origin.

CONSTRUCT

noun: /khan-struhkt/

Λ complex object assembled from various elements.

ΛLIEN CONSTRUCT

An extraterrestrial object built from various biological and mechanical parts.

Cryptogram Key

■ Follow these <u>4</u> steps to decode the name of the Alien Construct using the Decoder Key provided below.

1) Cut Out The Decoder Key Below

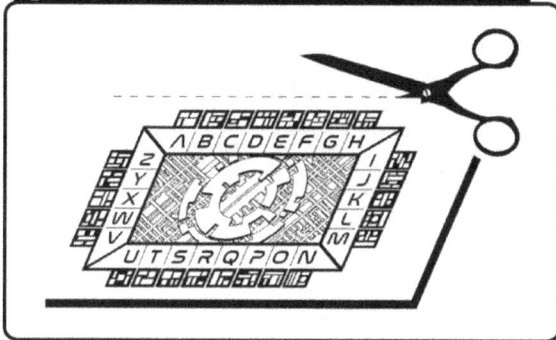

2) Match Key To Related Symbol

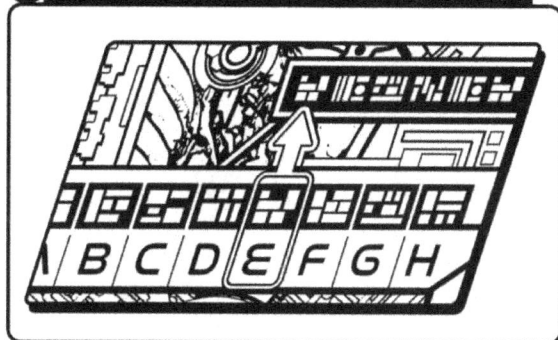

3) Enter Letter On Decode Page

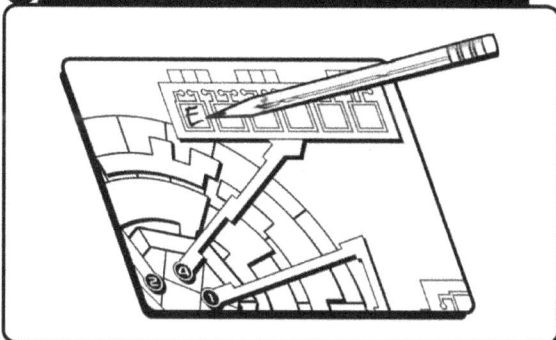

4) Write Out The Decoded Words

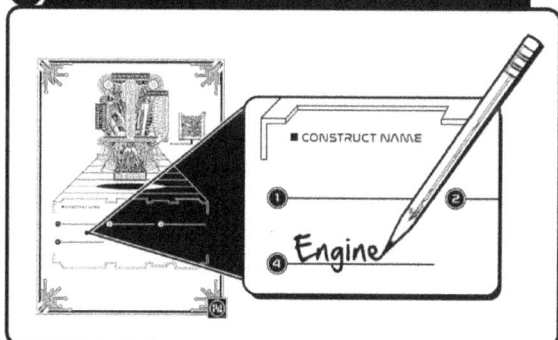

CONSTRUCT NAME

Engine

A B C D E F G H
Z Y X W V
I J K L M
U T S R Q P O N

Solving the Cryptogram

- In addition to the Decoder Key you can also decipher the name of the Alien Construct using your mobile device's QR Code scanner.

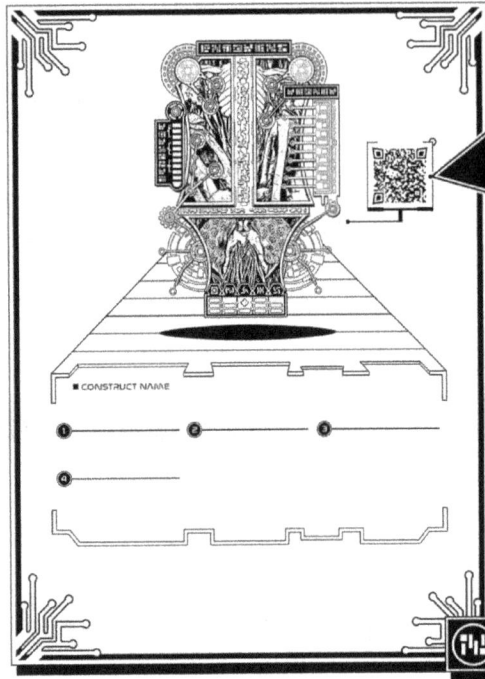

QR Code located on these pages.

CONSTRUCT NAME

As an added reference the corner of the page shows an alien symbol with its decoded letter.

- The decoded name of the Alien Construct is also listed - upside down - on the last few pages of this book.

Art Medium Testing Page

■ Test your coloring medium in the boxes below.

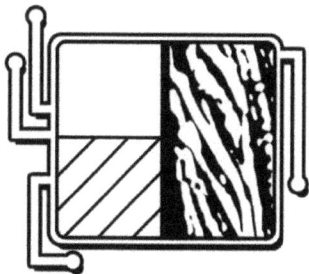

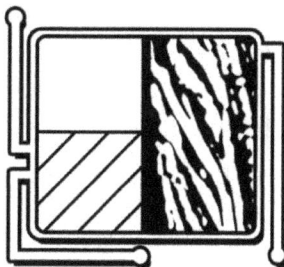

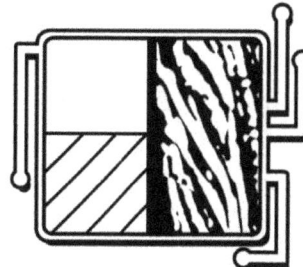

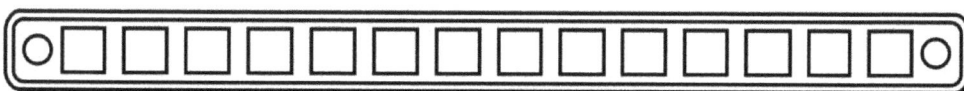

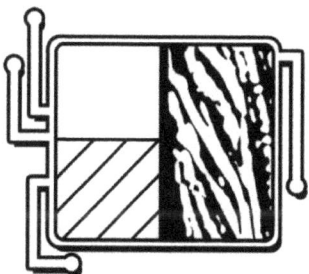

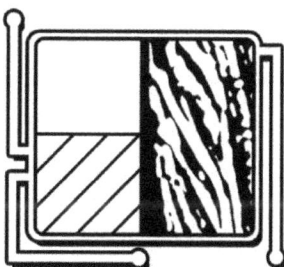

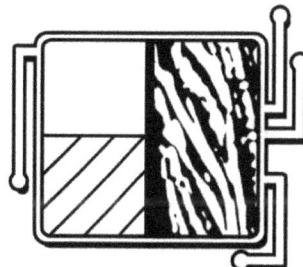

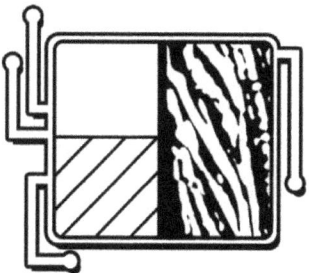

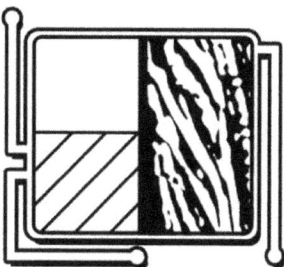

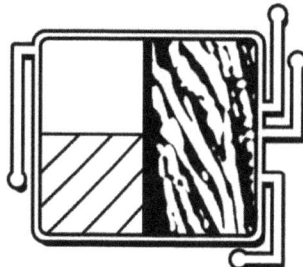

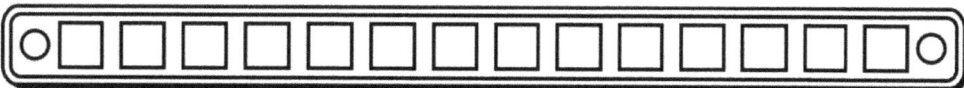

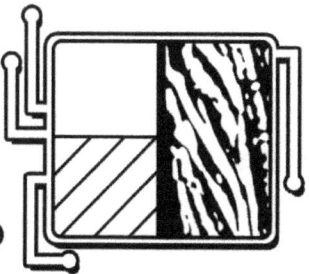

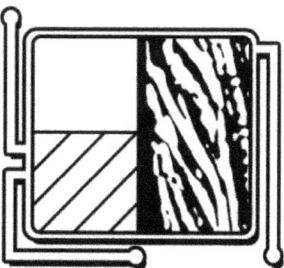

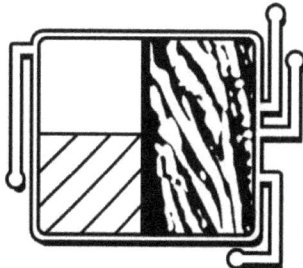

Was There Bleed-Through?

■ If so, put scrap paper under the page you are coloring.

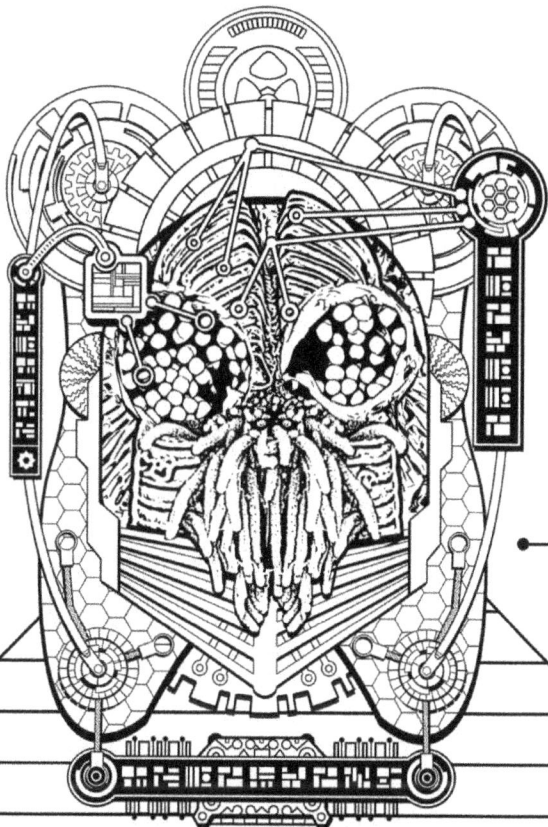

■ CONSTRUCT NAME

1 ——————————— 2 *synthetic* 3 ———————————

4 ———————————

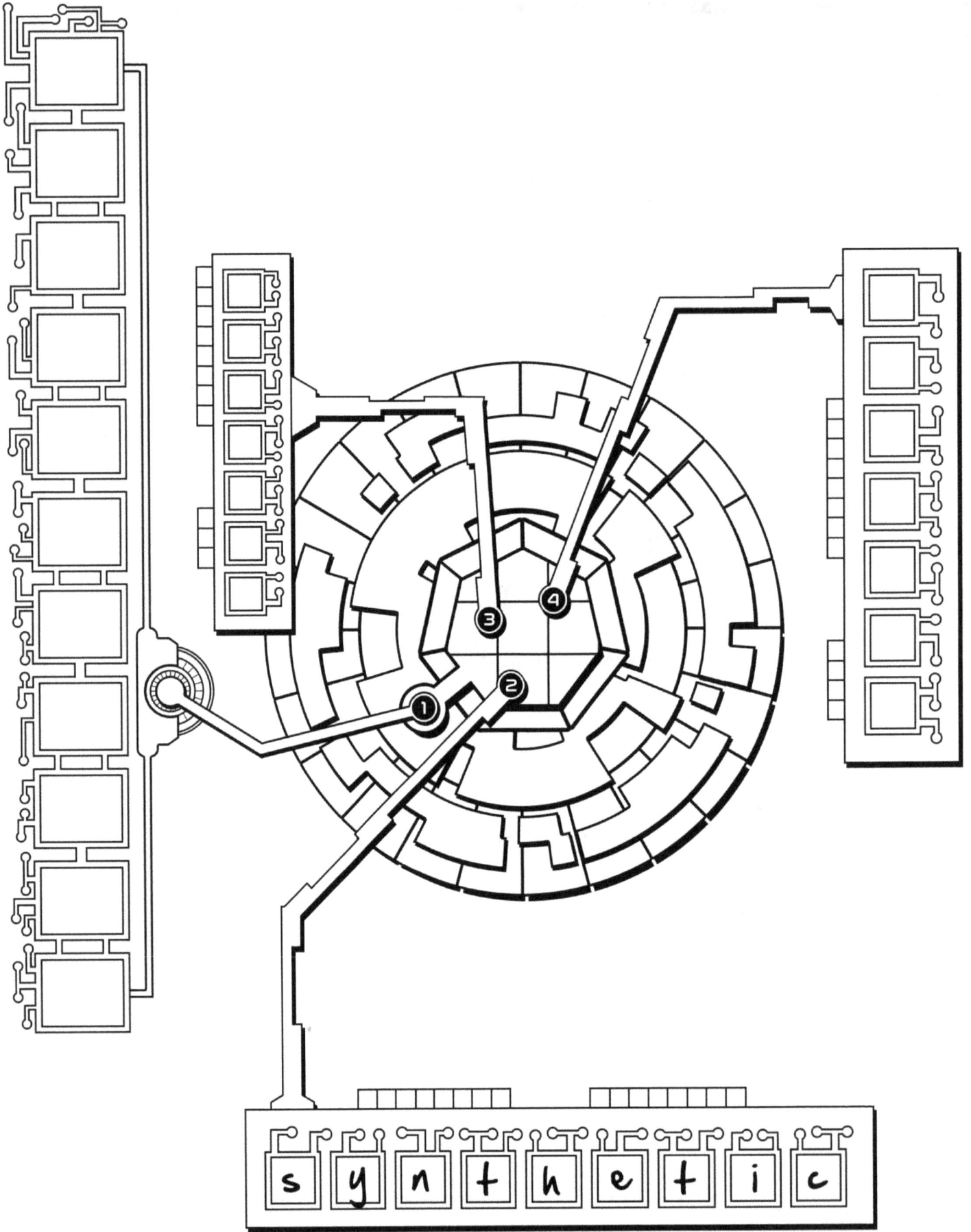

synthetic

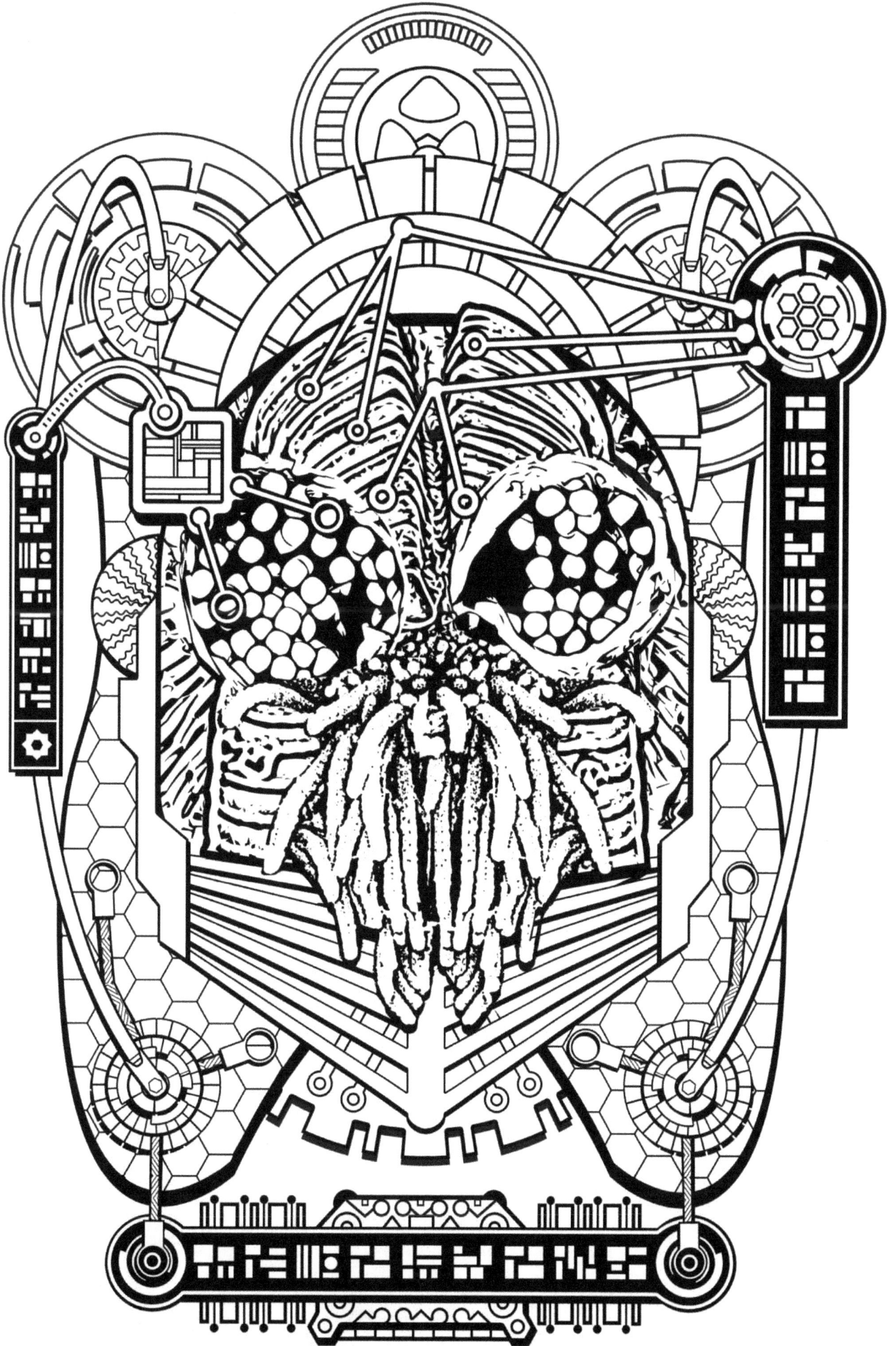

■ CONSTRUCT NAME

①
②
③

④

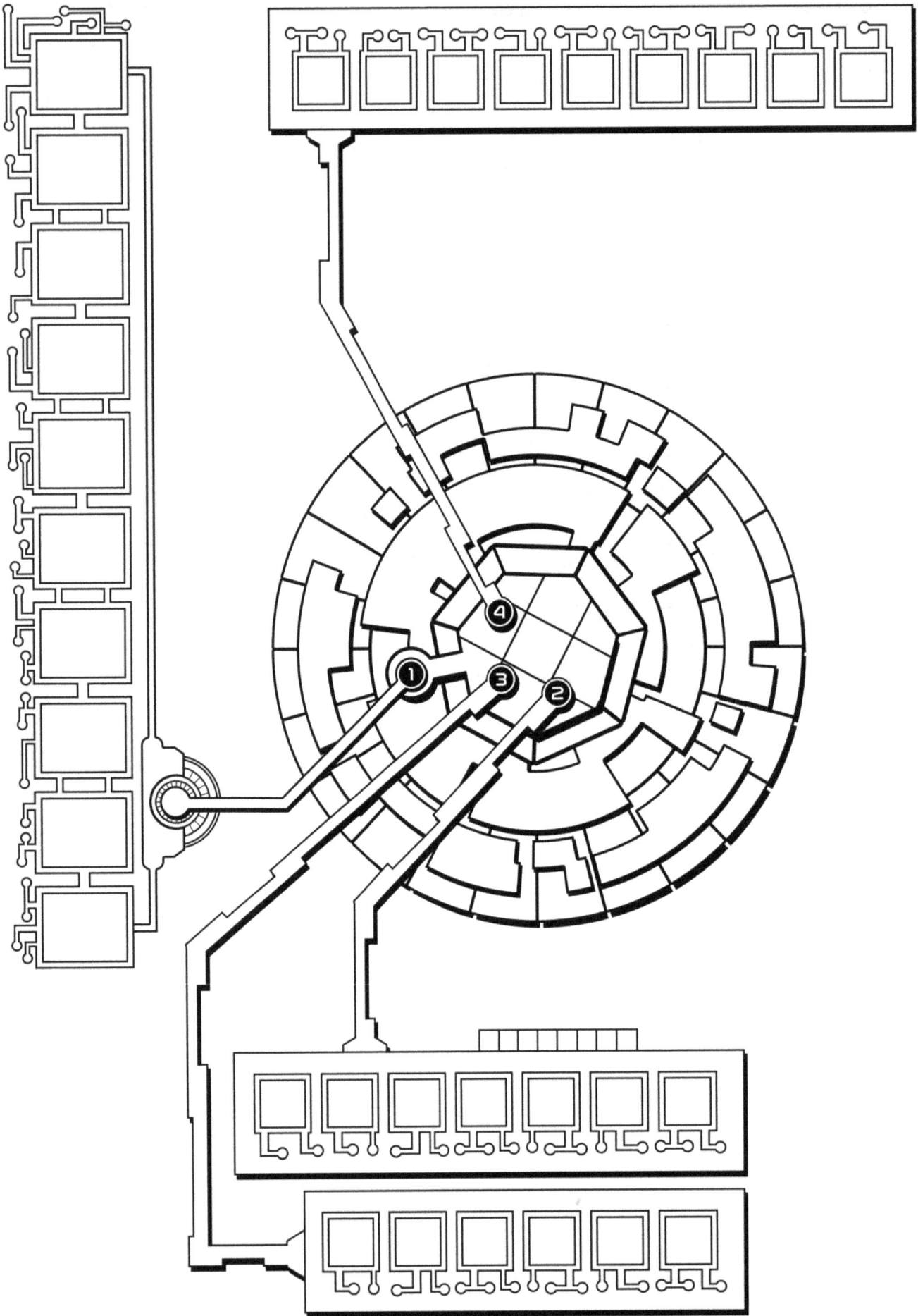

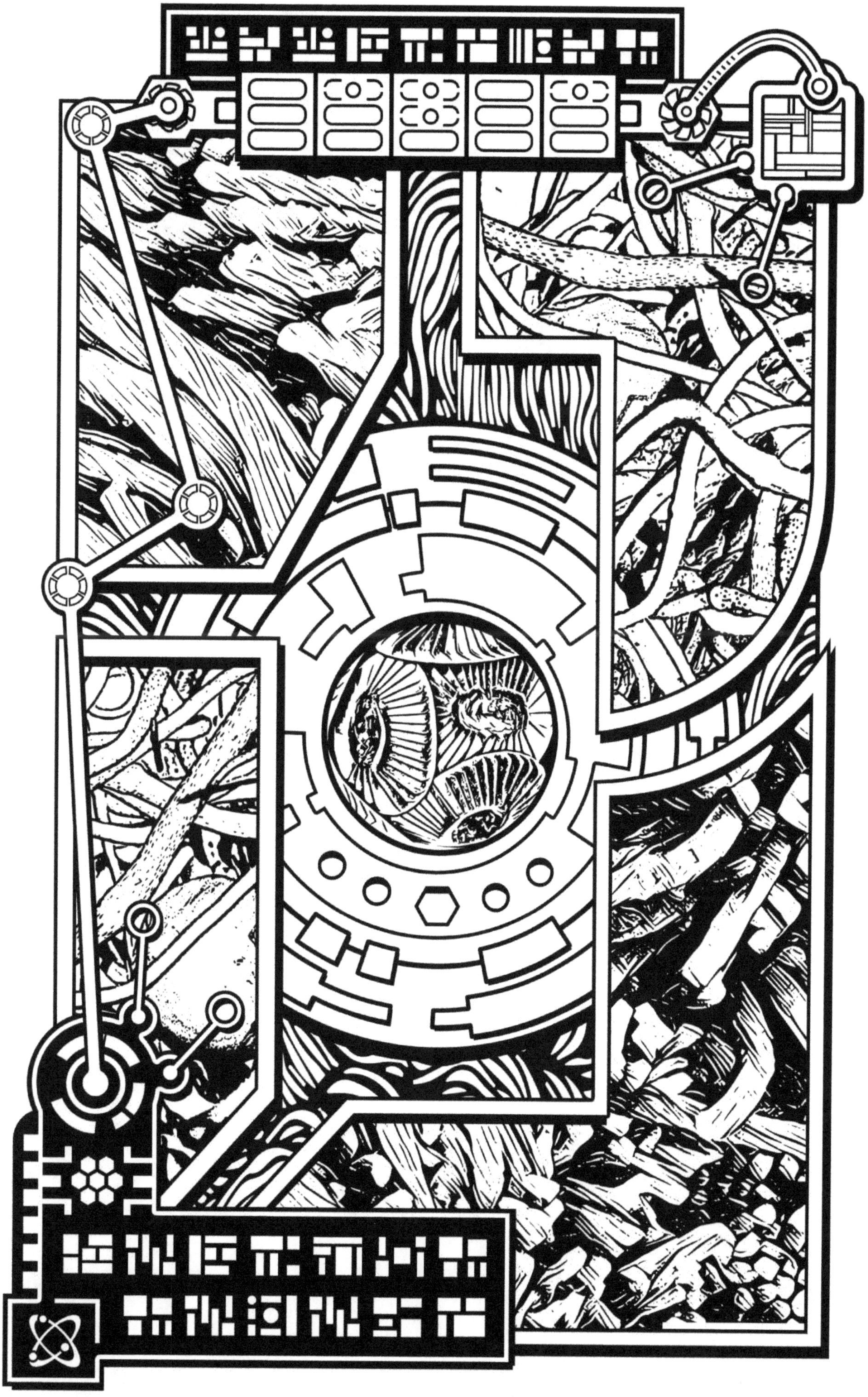

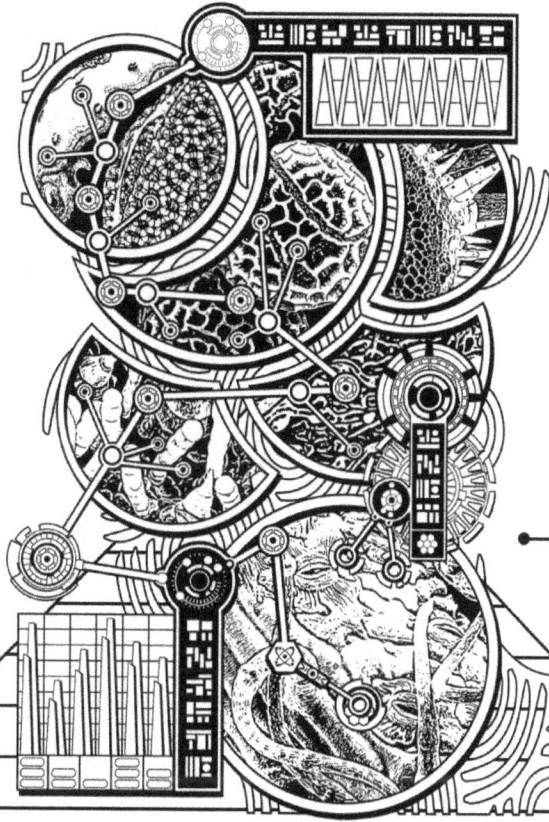

■ CONSTRUCT NAME

① ──────────── ② ──────────── ③ ────────────

④ ────────────

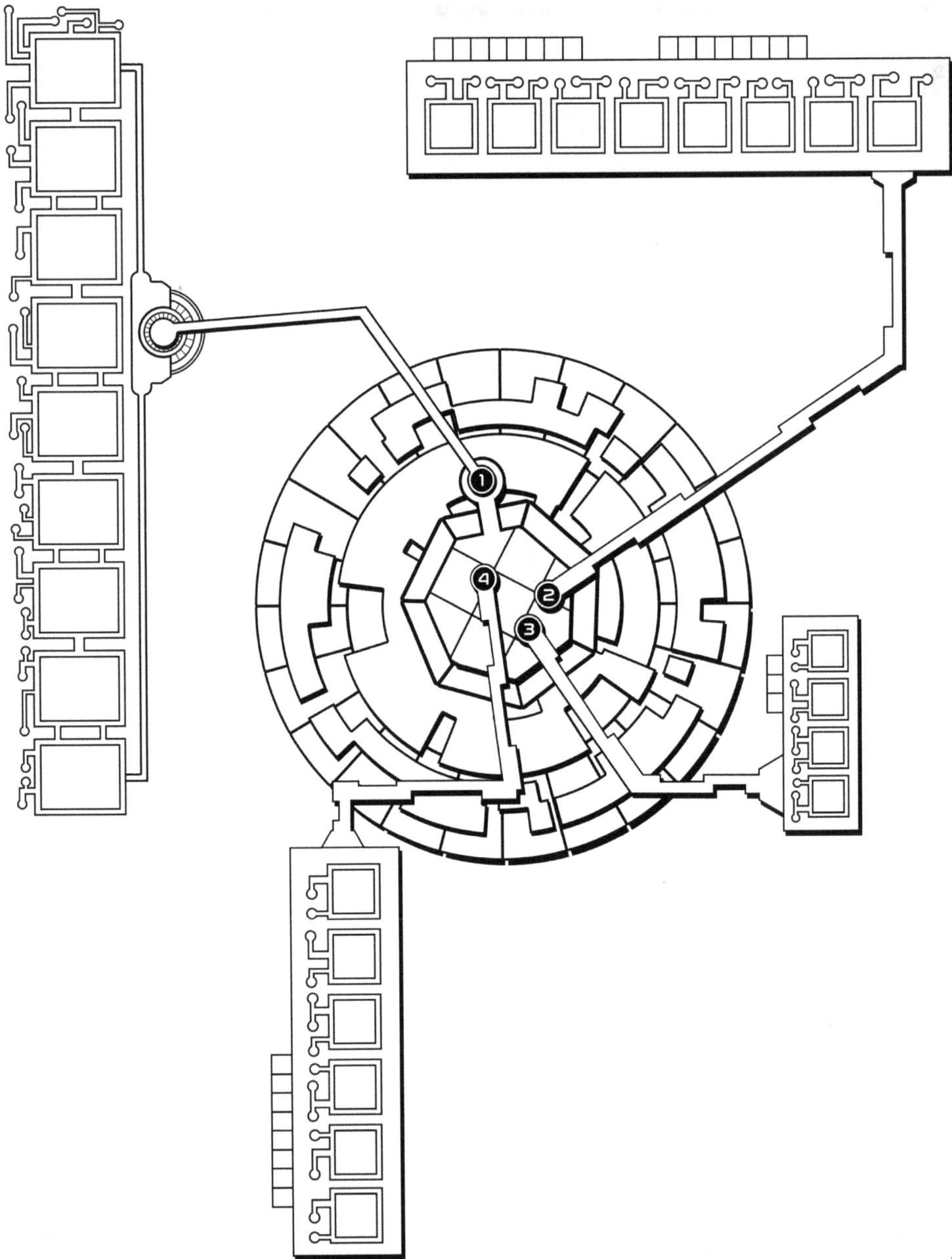

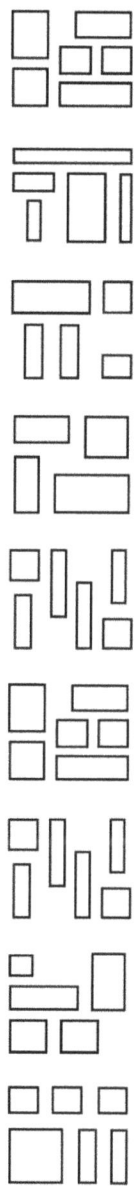

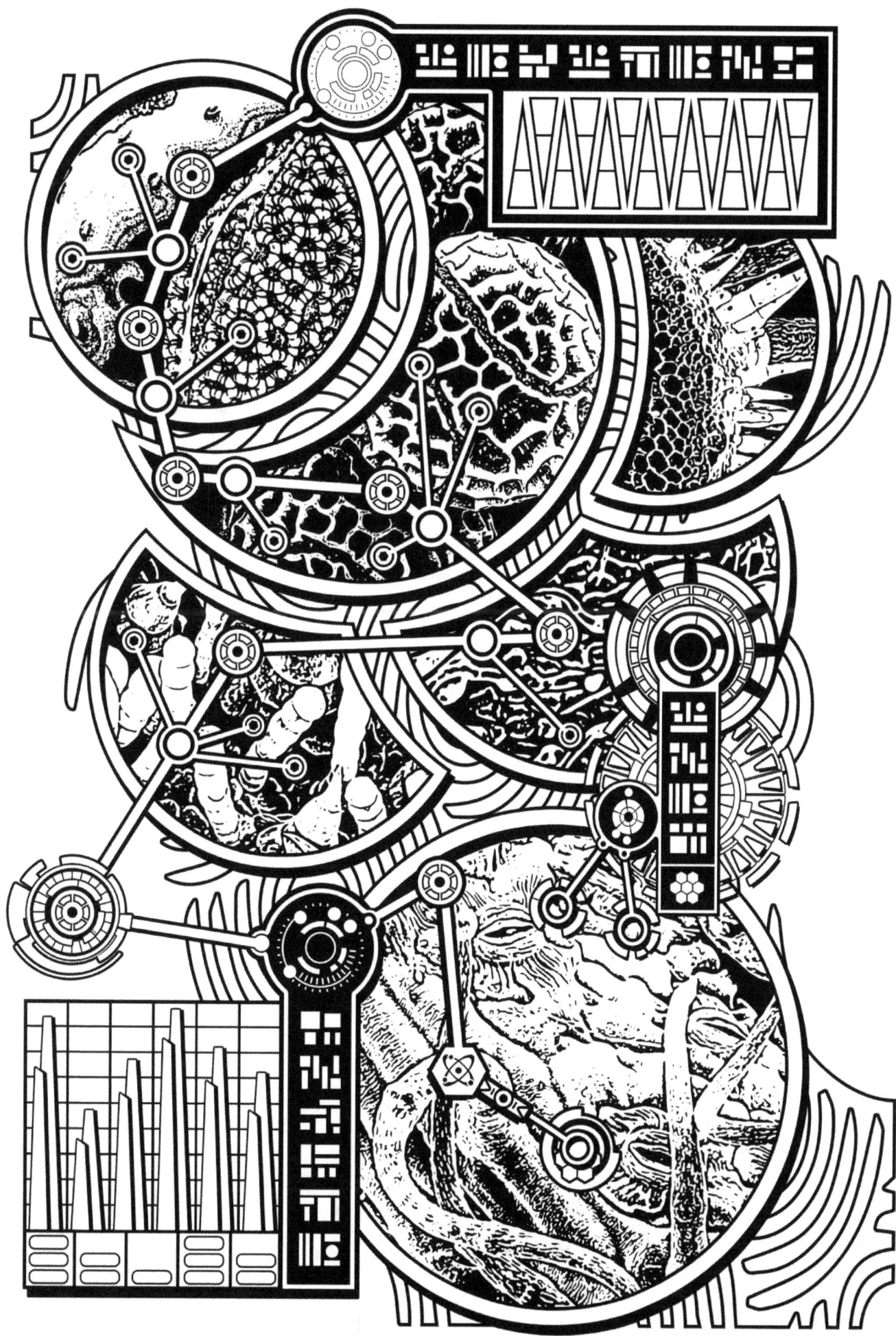

■ CONSTRUCT NAME

1 ——————————— 2 ——————————— 3 ———————————

4 ——————————— 5 ———————————

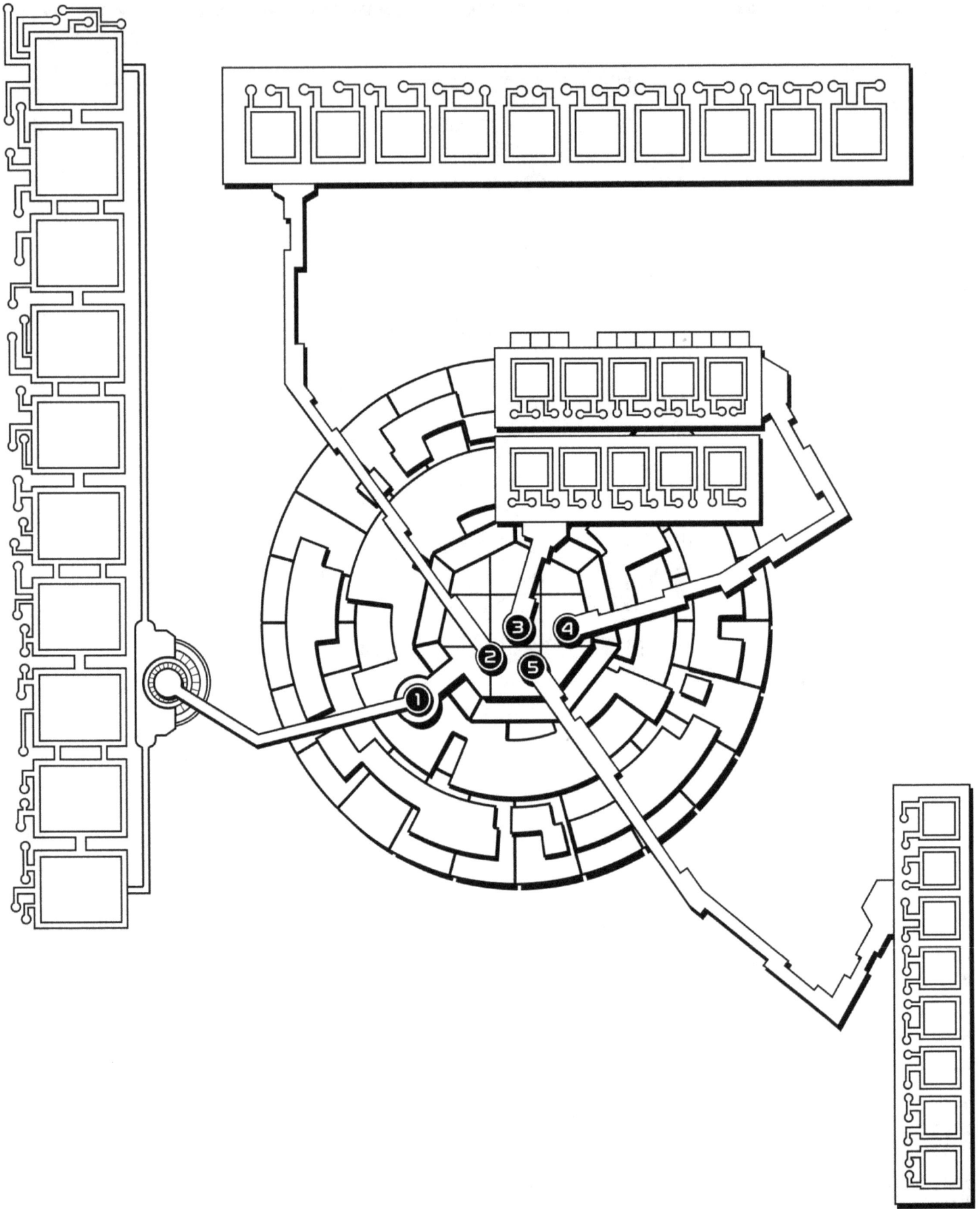

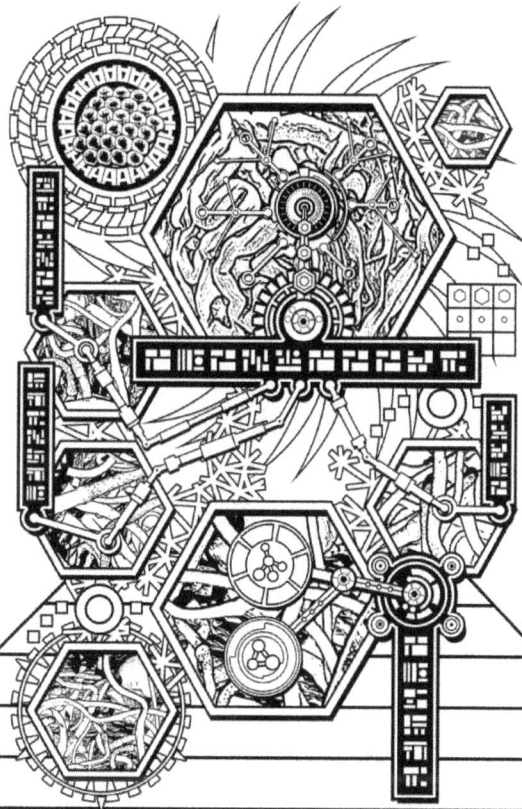

■ CONSTRUCT NAME

① ———————————— ② ———————————— ③ ————————————

④ ———————————— ⑤ ———————————— ⑥ ————————————

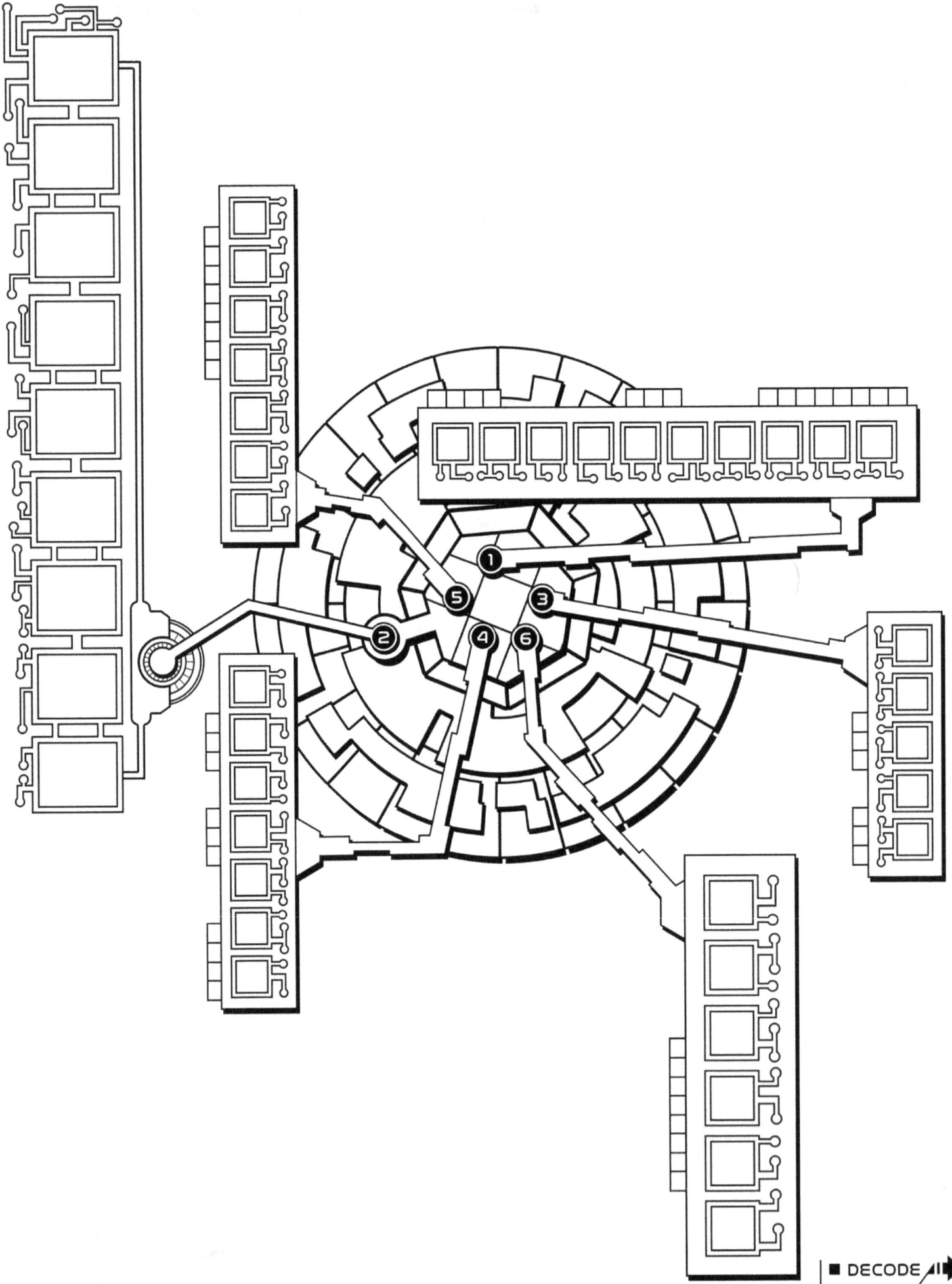

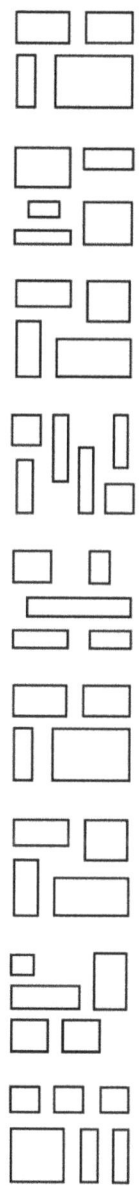

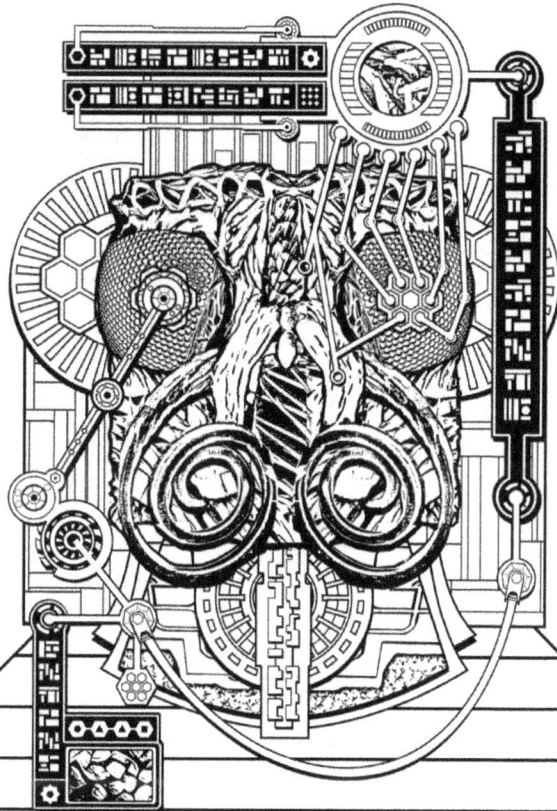

■ CONSTRUCT NAME

① ————————— ② ————————— ③ —————————

④ ————————— ⑤ —————————

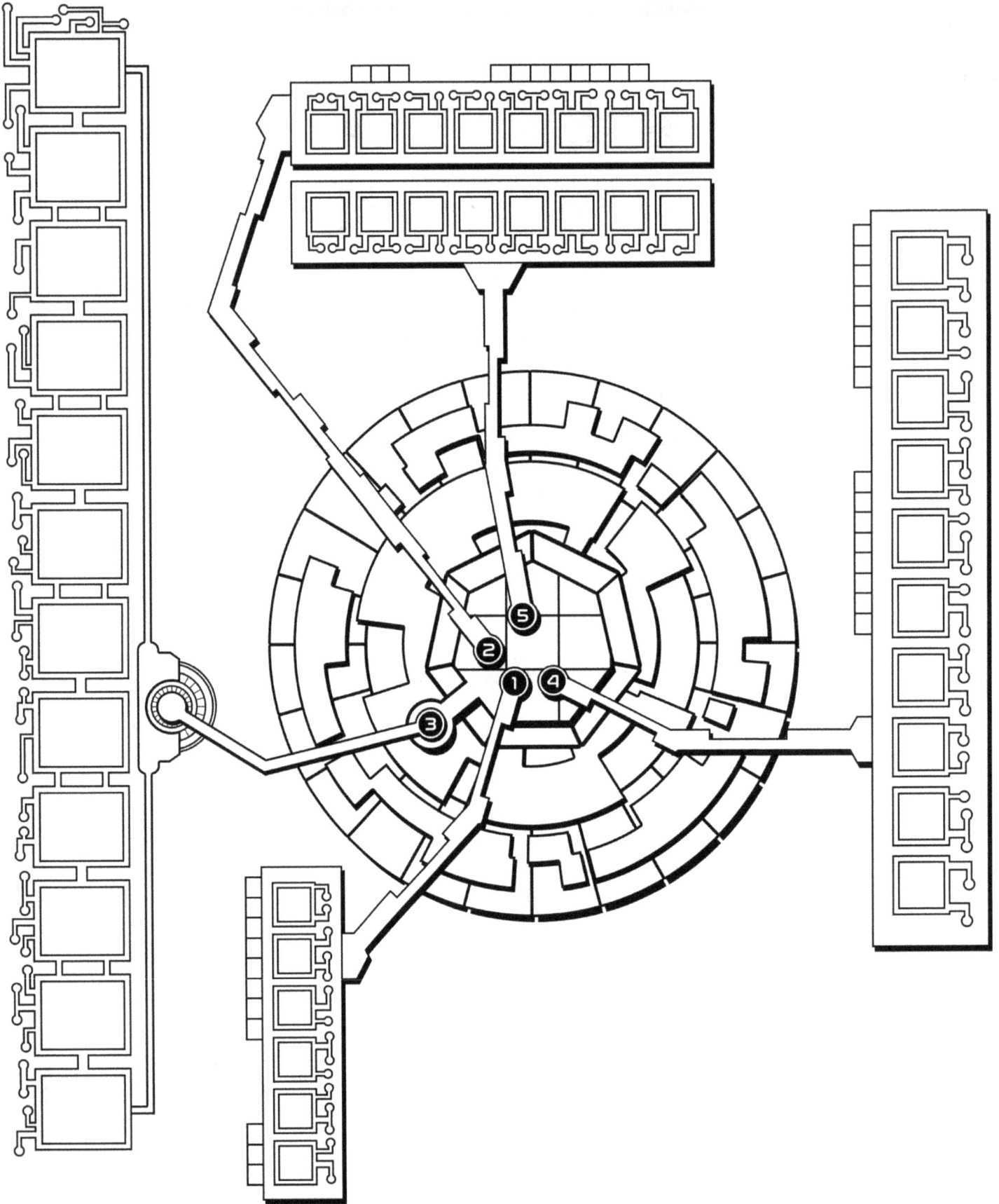

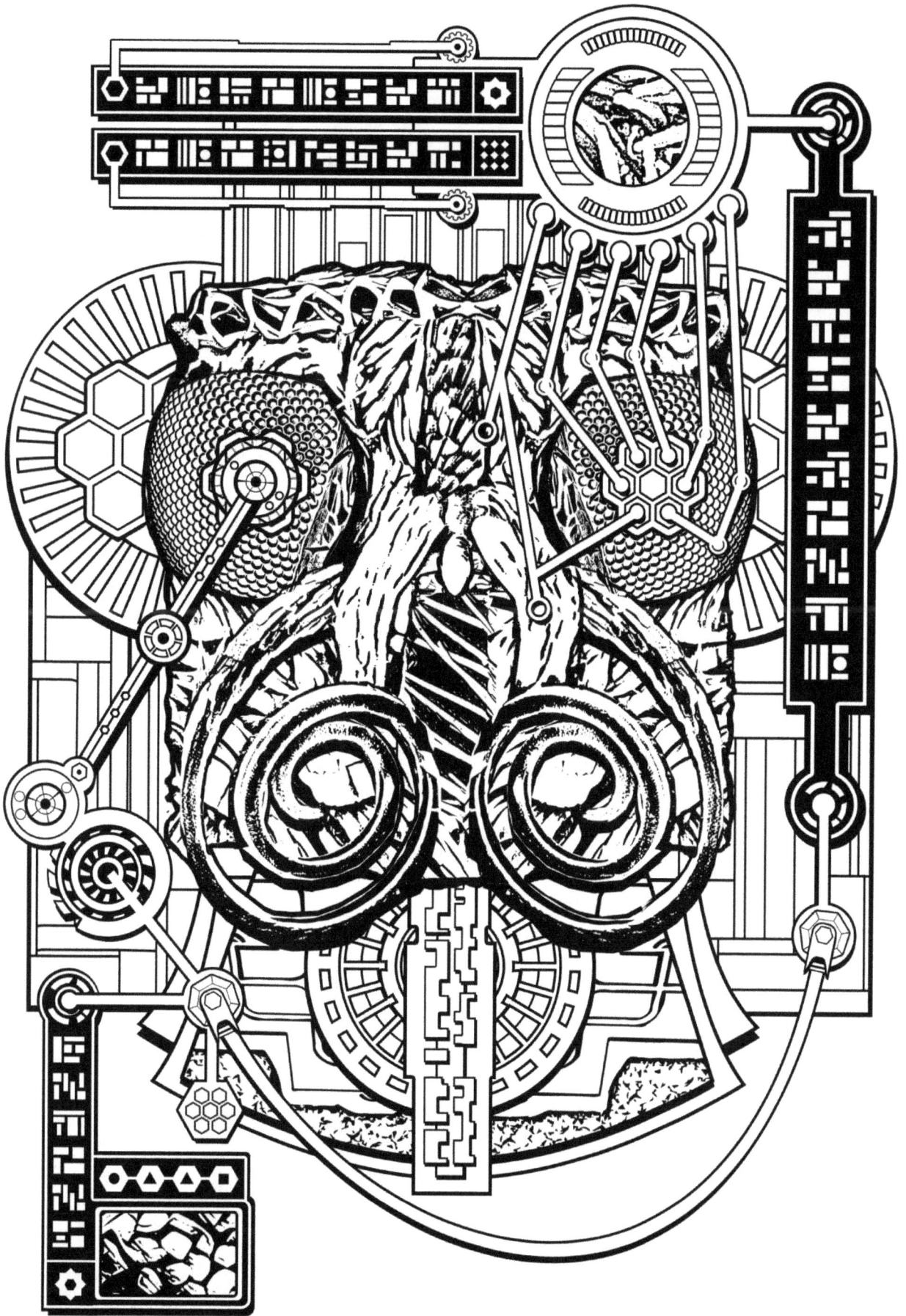

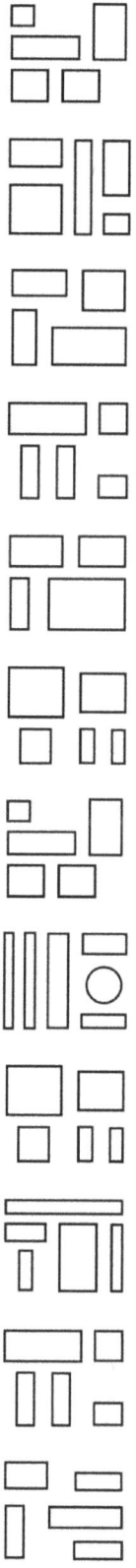

■ CONSTRUCT NAME

1
2
3
4
5

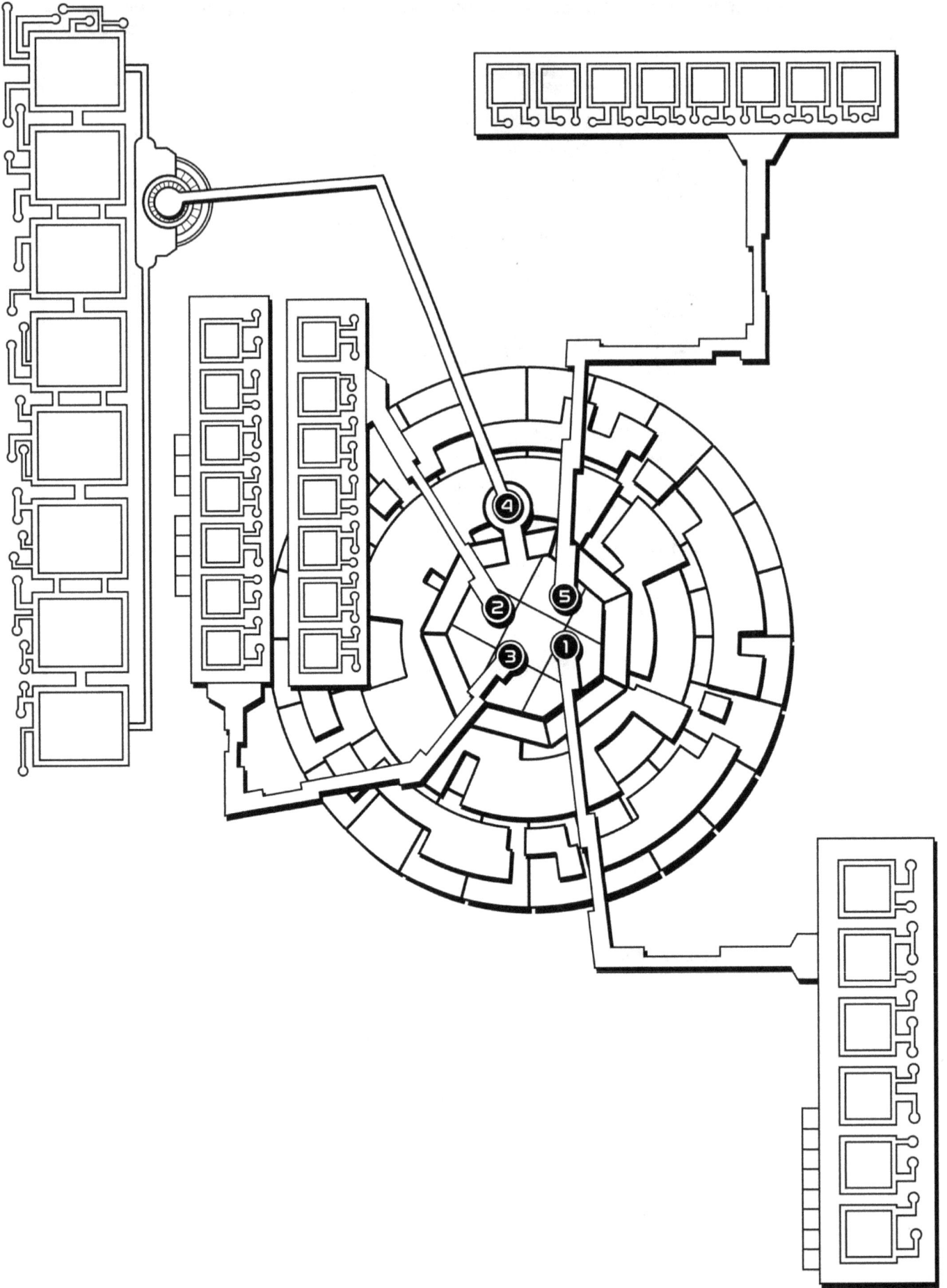

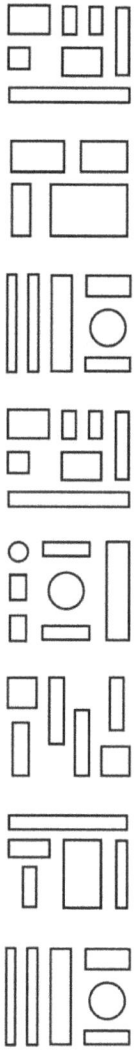

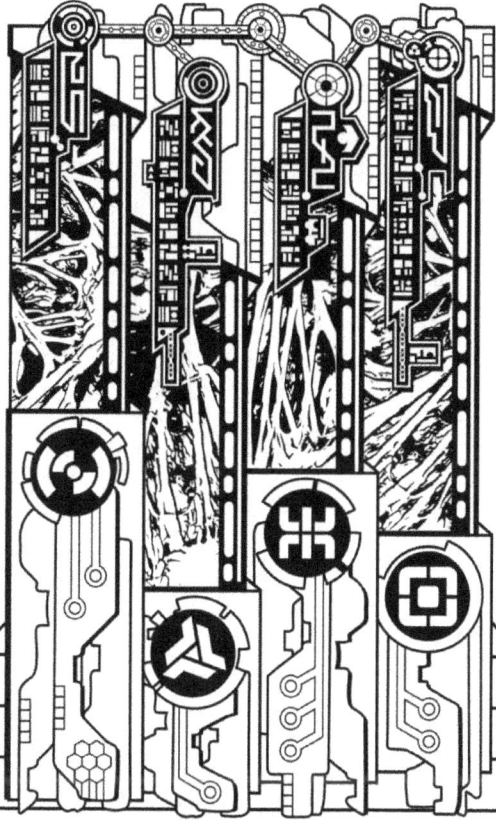

■ CONSTRUCT NAME

① ——————————— ② ——————————— ③ ———————————

④ ——————————— ⑤ ———————————

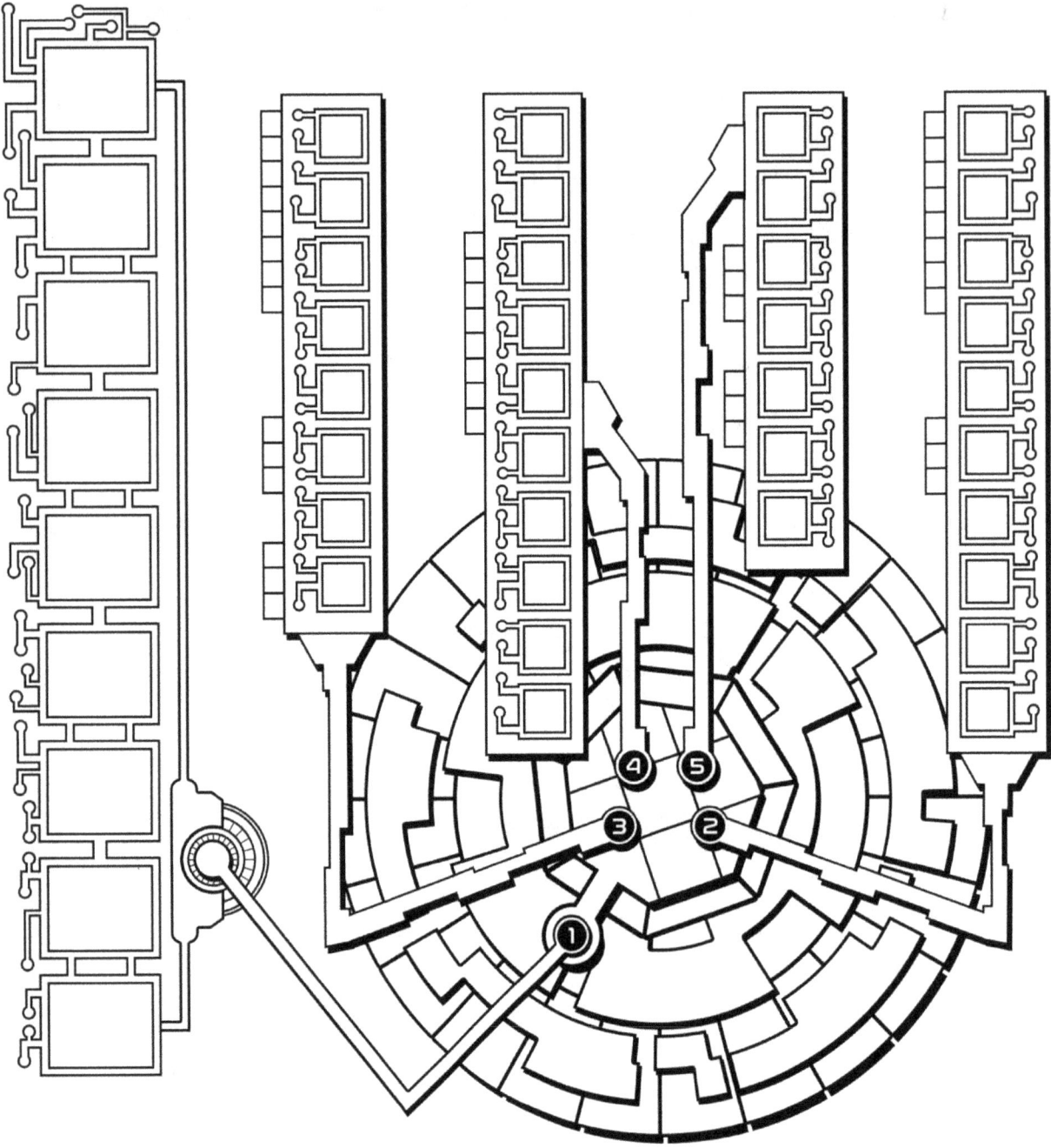

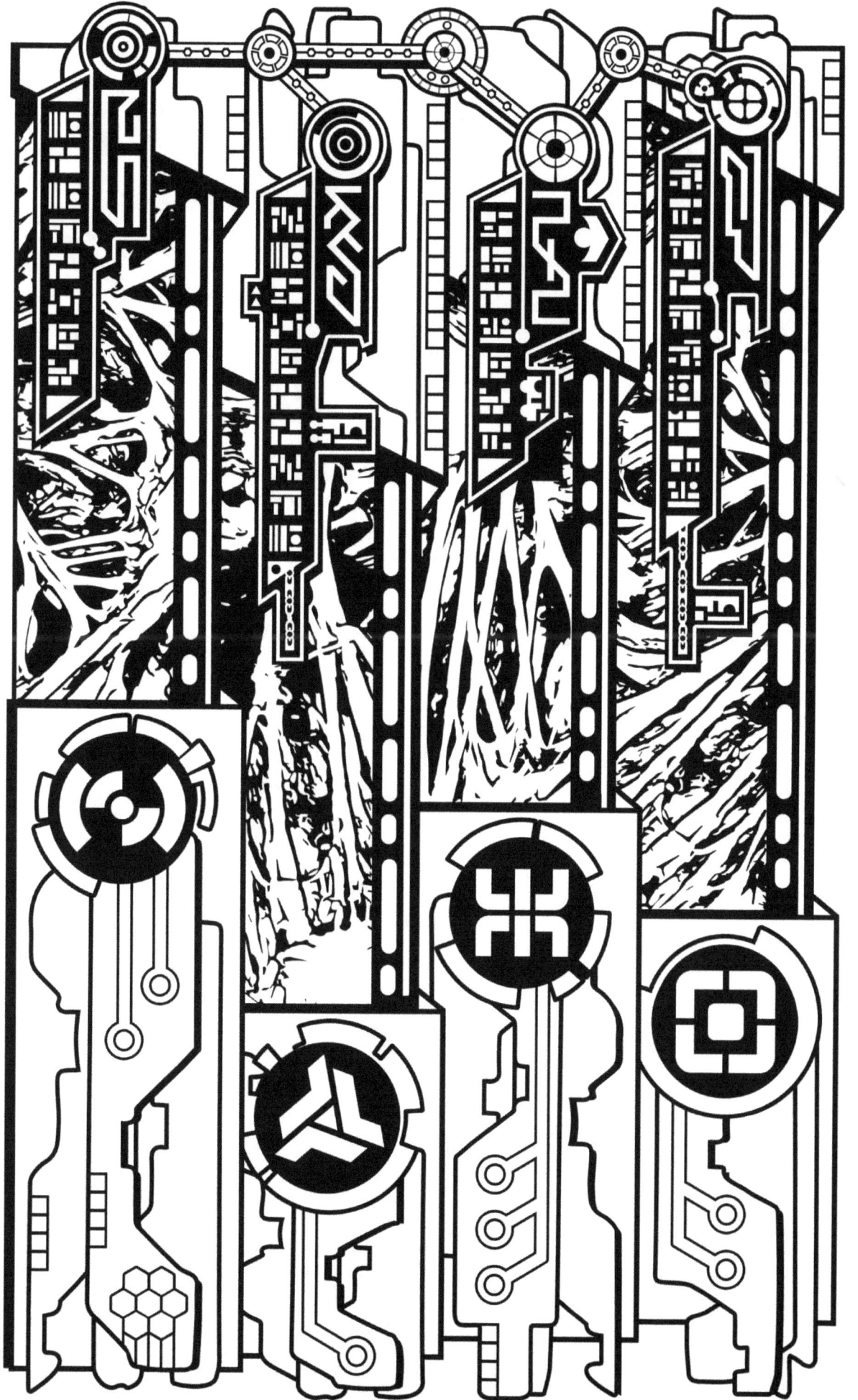

■ CONSTRUCT NAME

① ──────────────── ② ──────────────── ③ ────────────

④ ────────────────

I

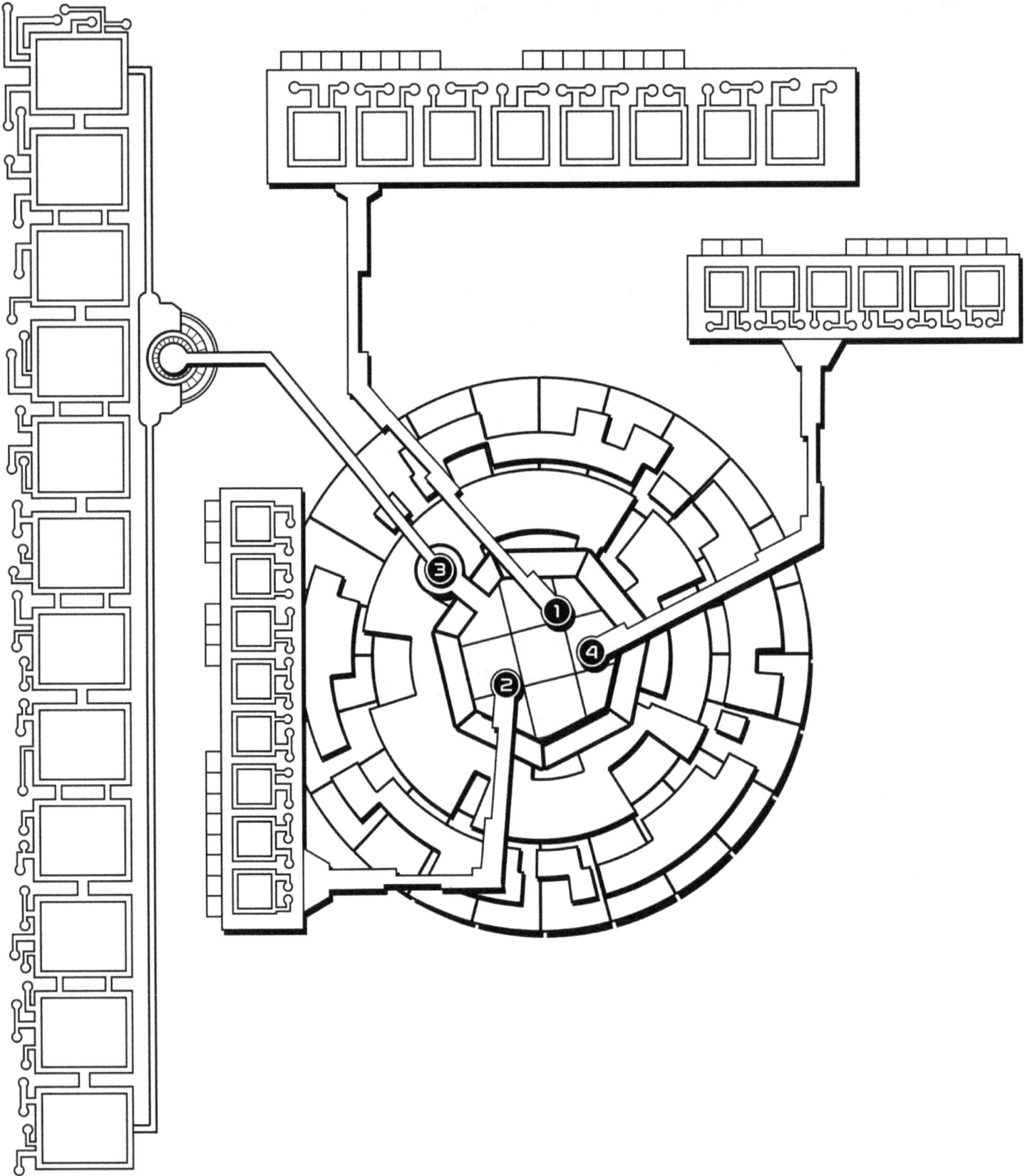

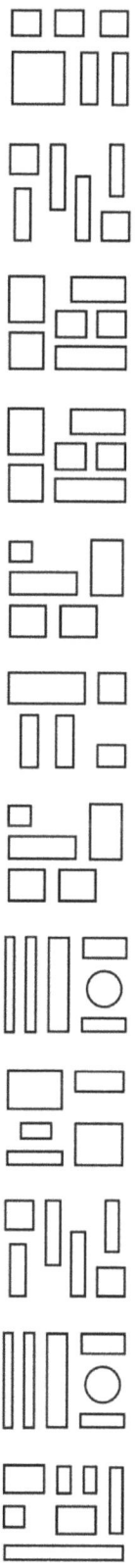

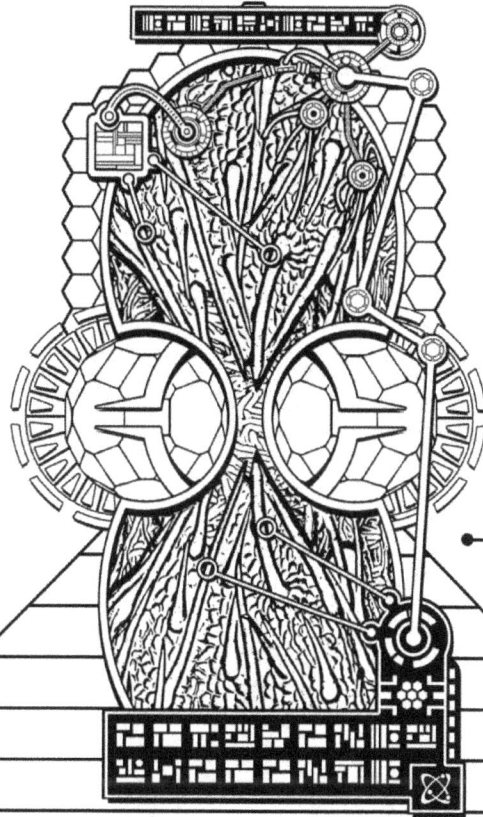

■ CONSTRUCT NAME

① —————————————— ② —————————————— ③ ——————————————

④ ——————————————

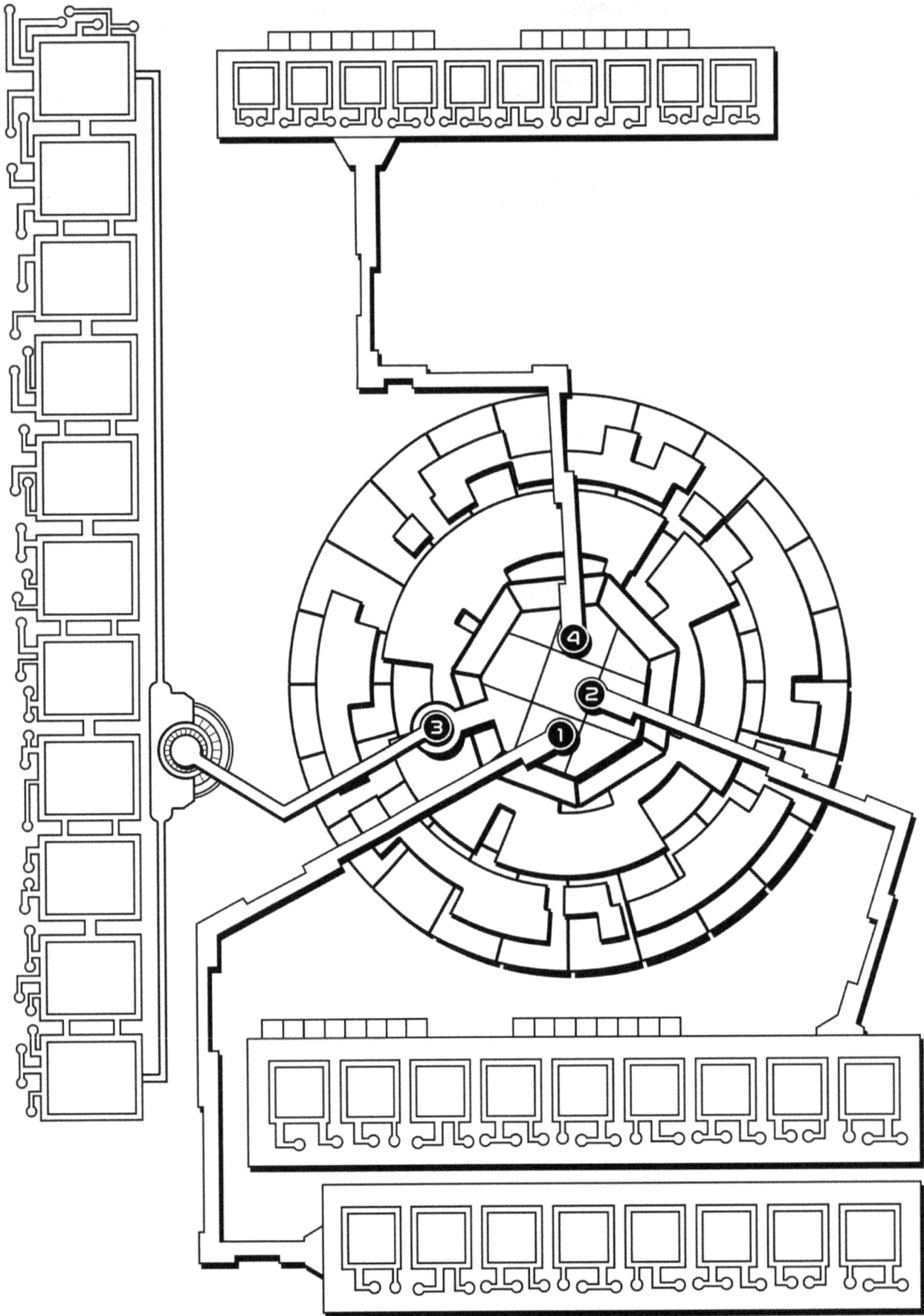

■ DECODE ◢▮▶

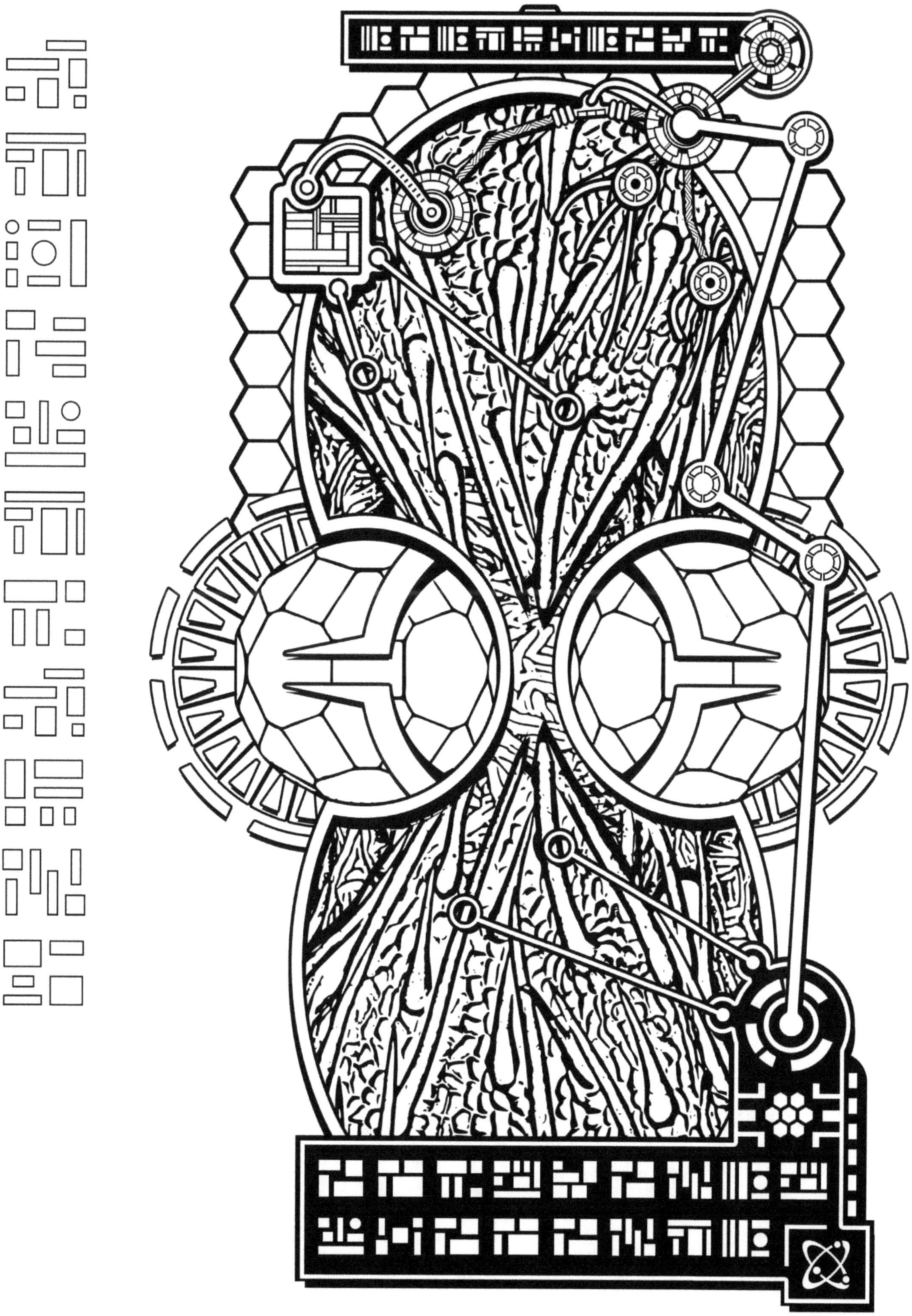

■ CONSTRUCT NAME

1 ——————————————— **2** ——————————————— **3** ———————

4 ———————————————

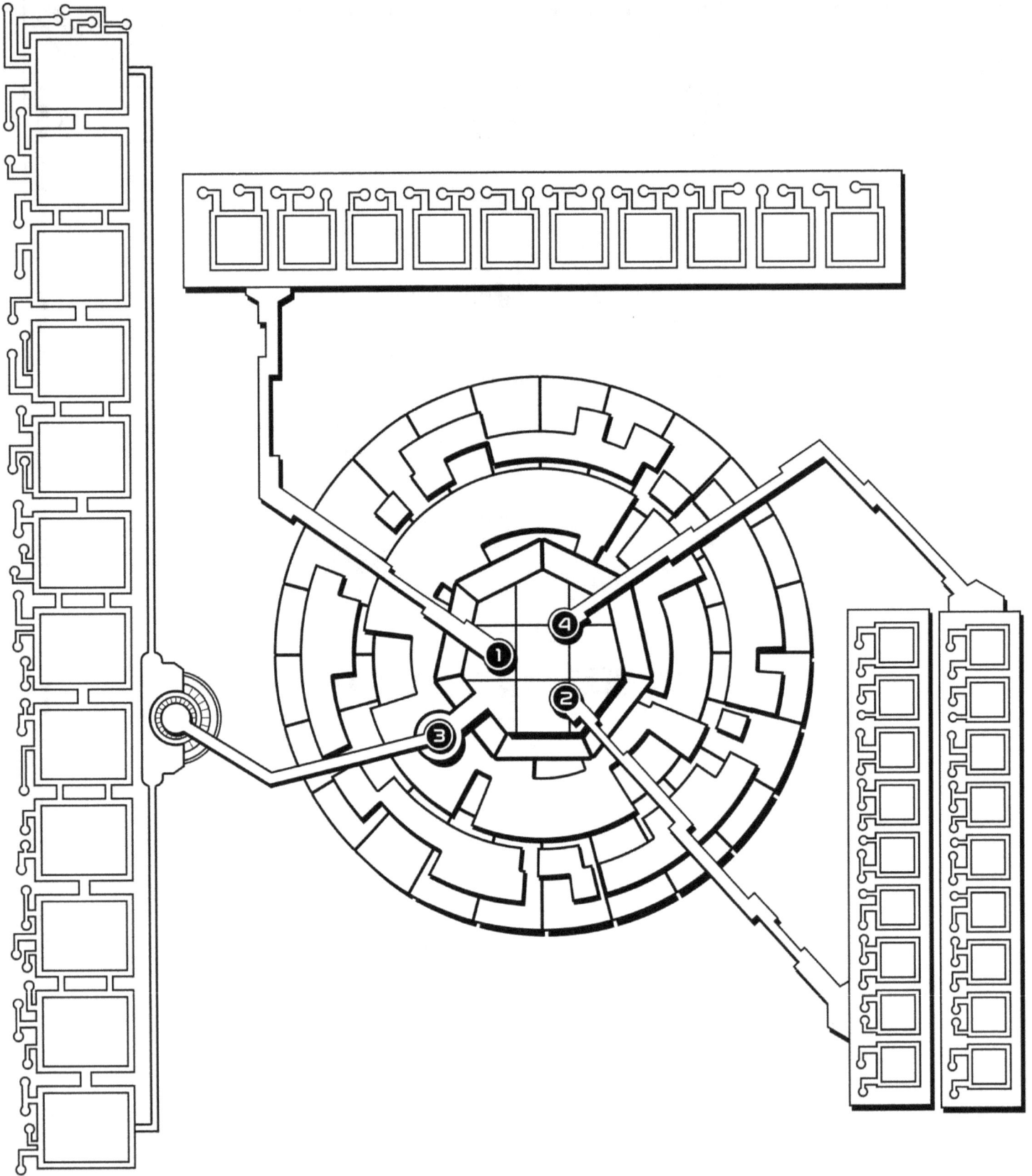

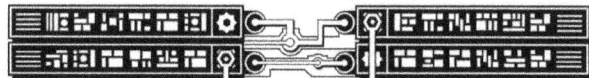

■ CONSTRUCT NAME

① —————————————— ② —————————————— ③ ——————————————

④ —————————————— ⑤ —————————————— ⑥ ——————————————

⑦ ——————————————

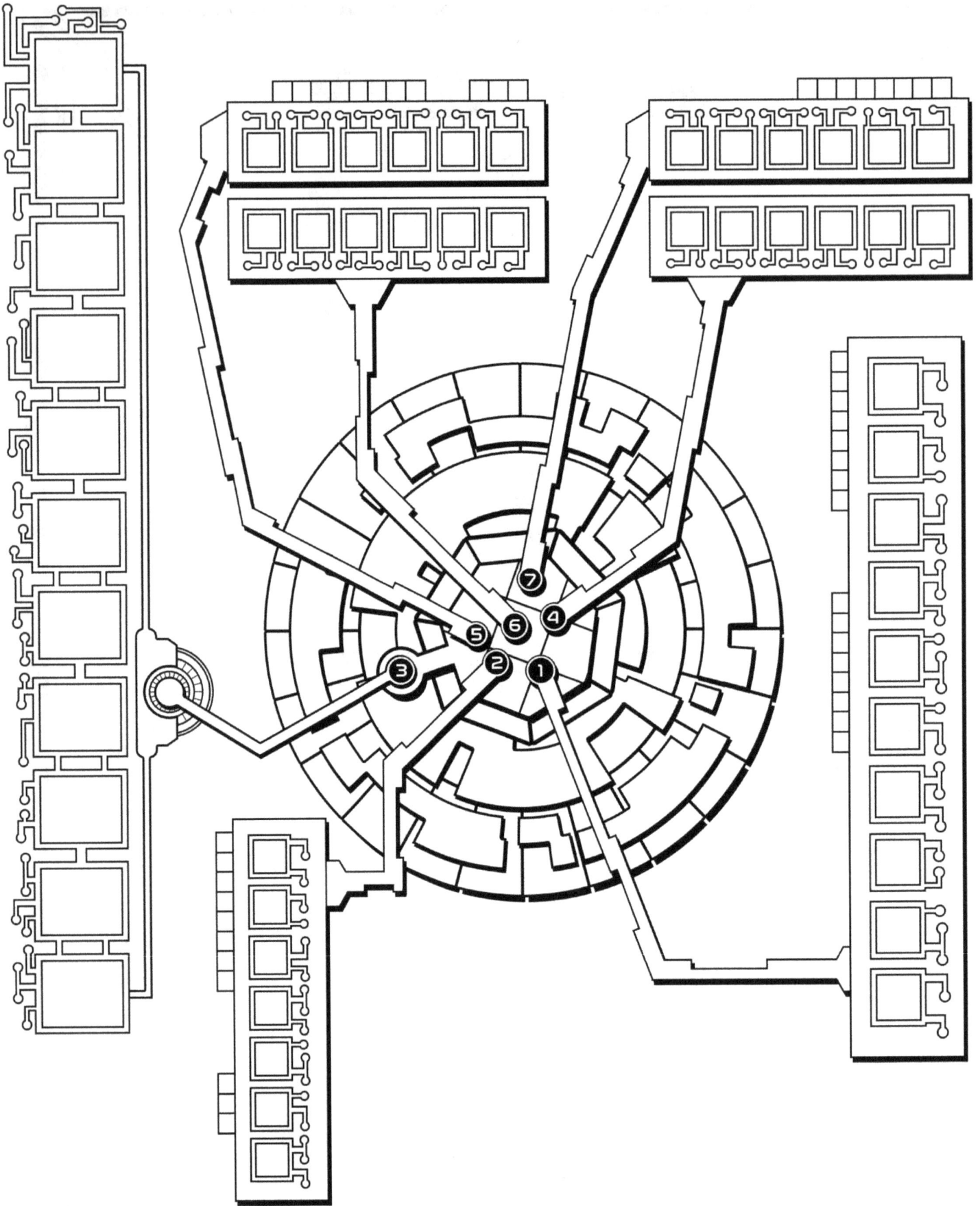

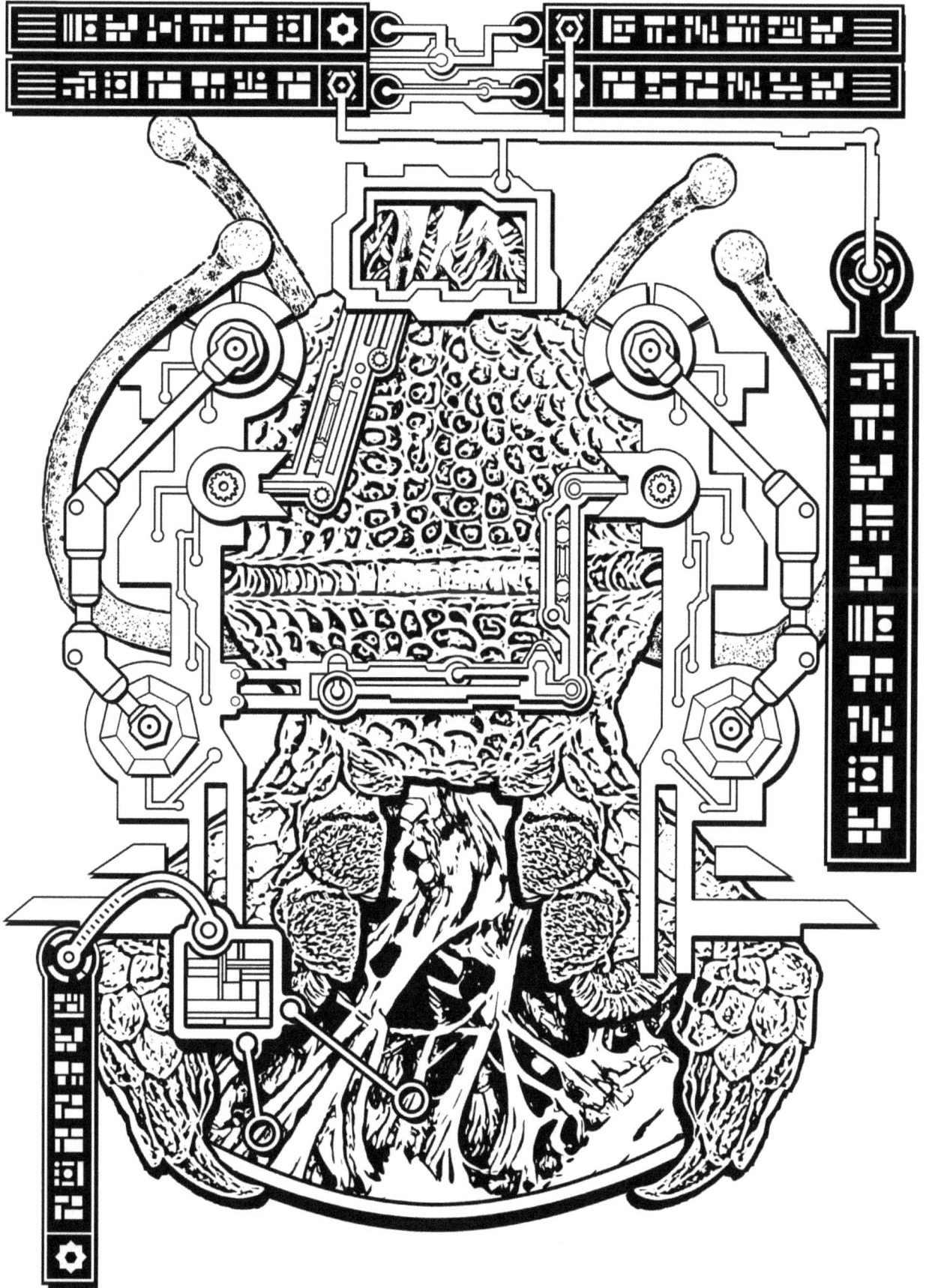

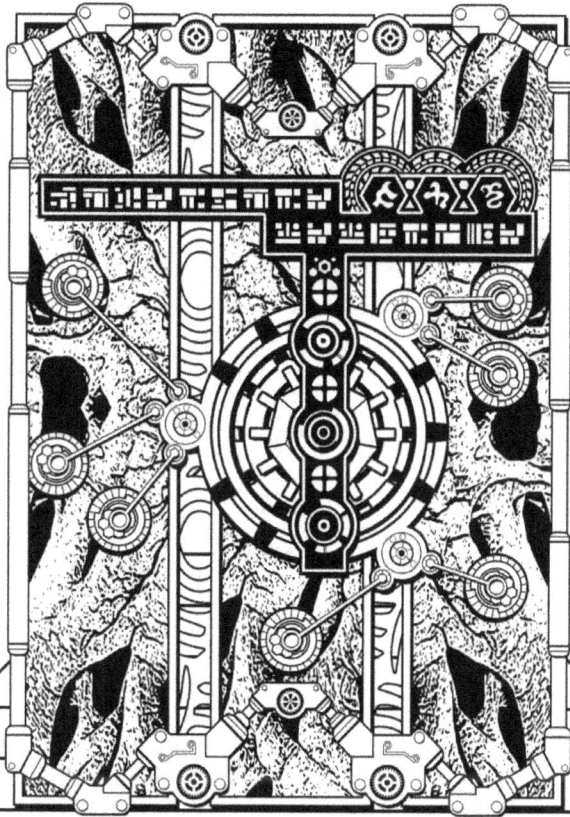

■ CONSTRUCT NAME

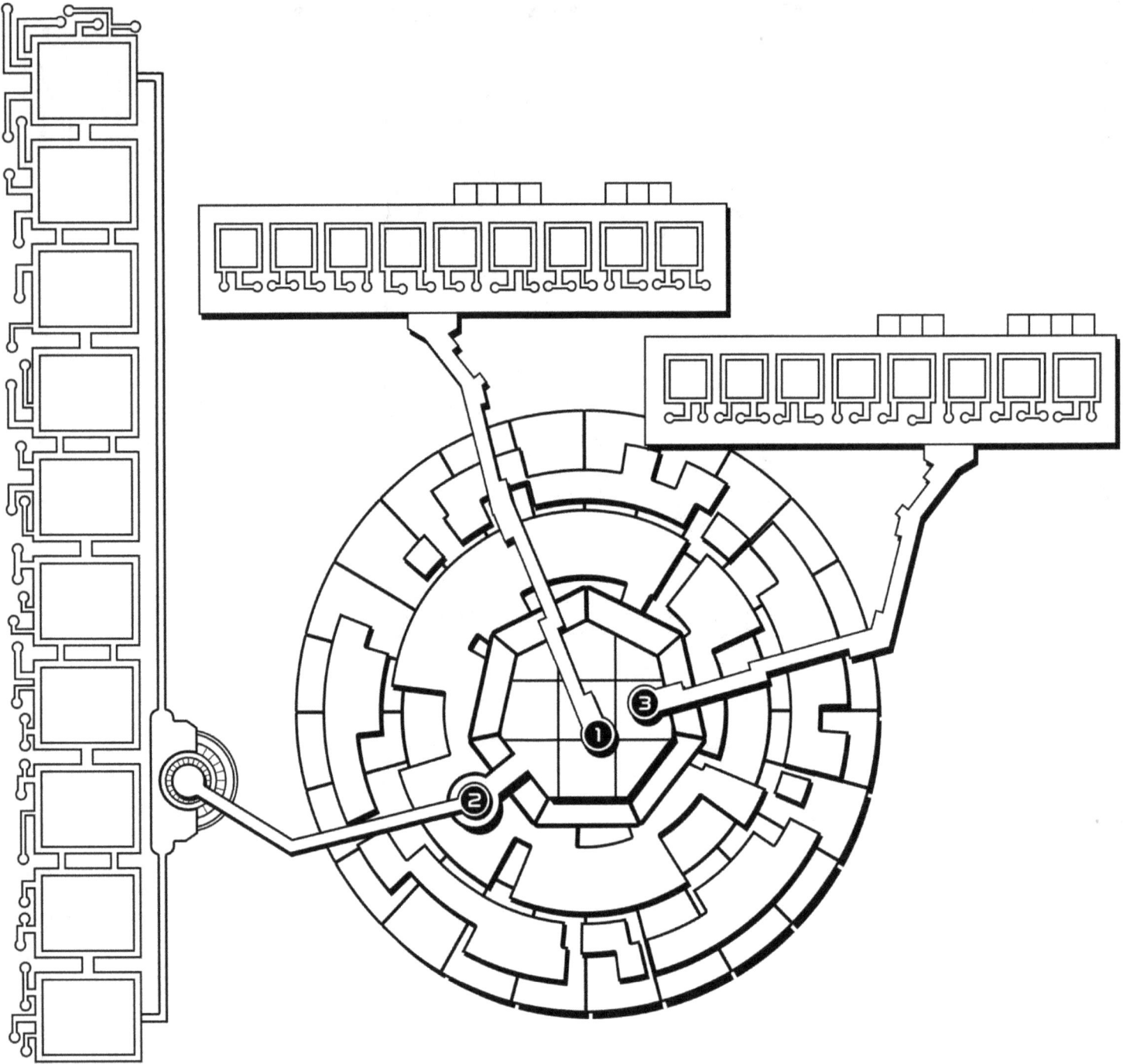

■ CONSTRUCT NAME

1 ——————————— 2 ——————— 3 ——————

4 ——————————— 5 ——————

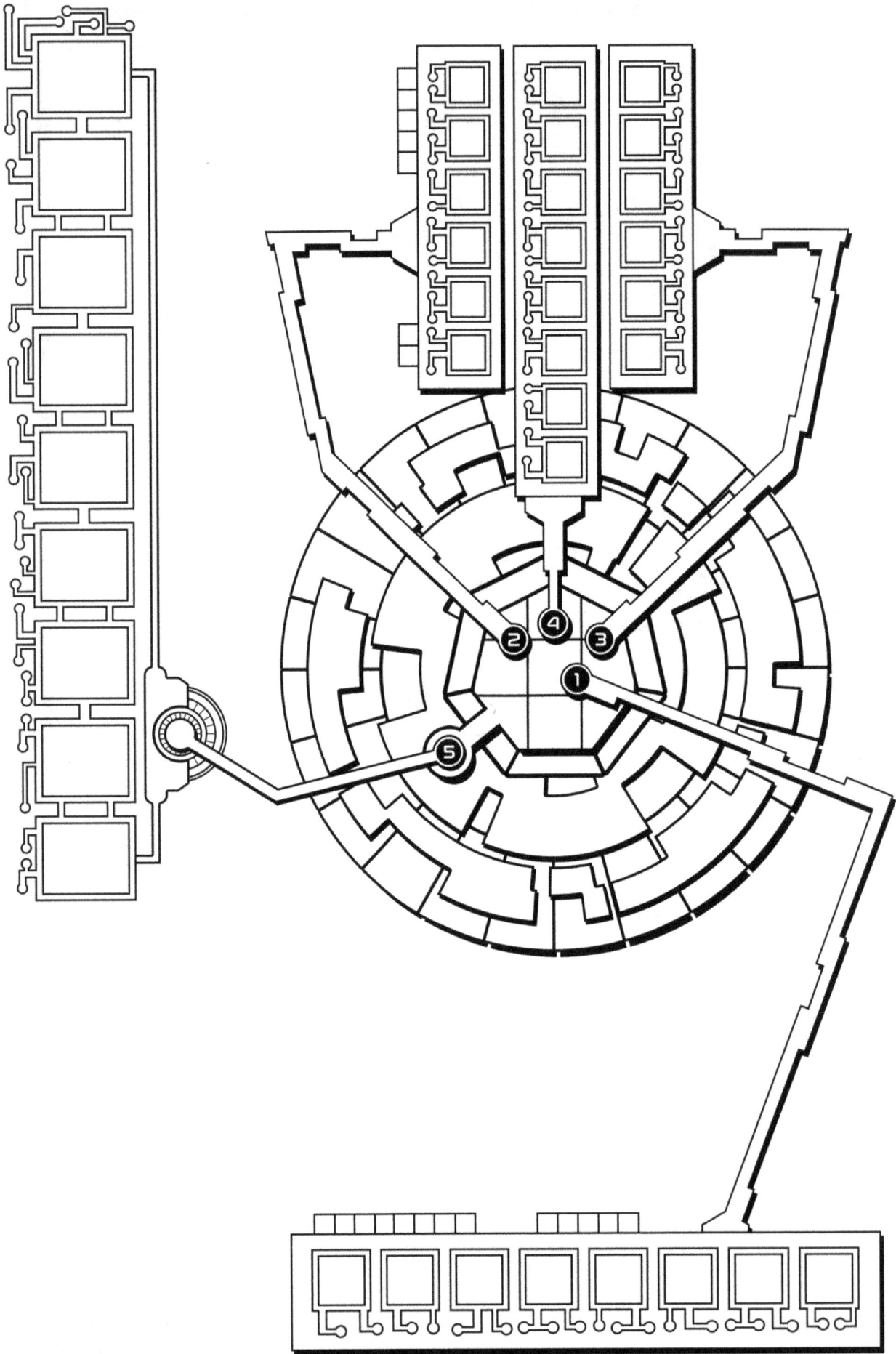

■ CONSTRUCT NAME

1
2
3

4
5

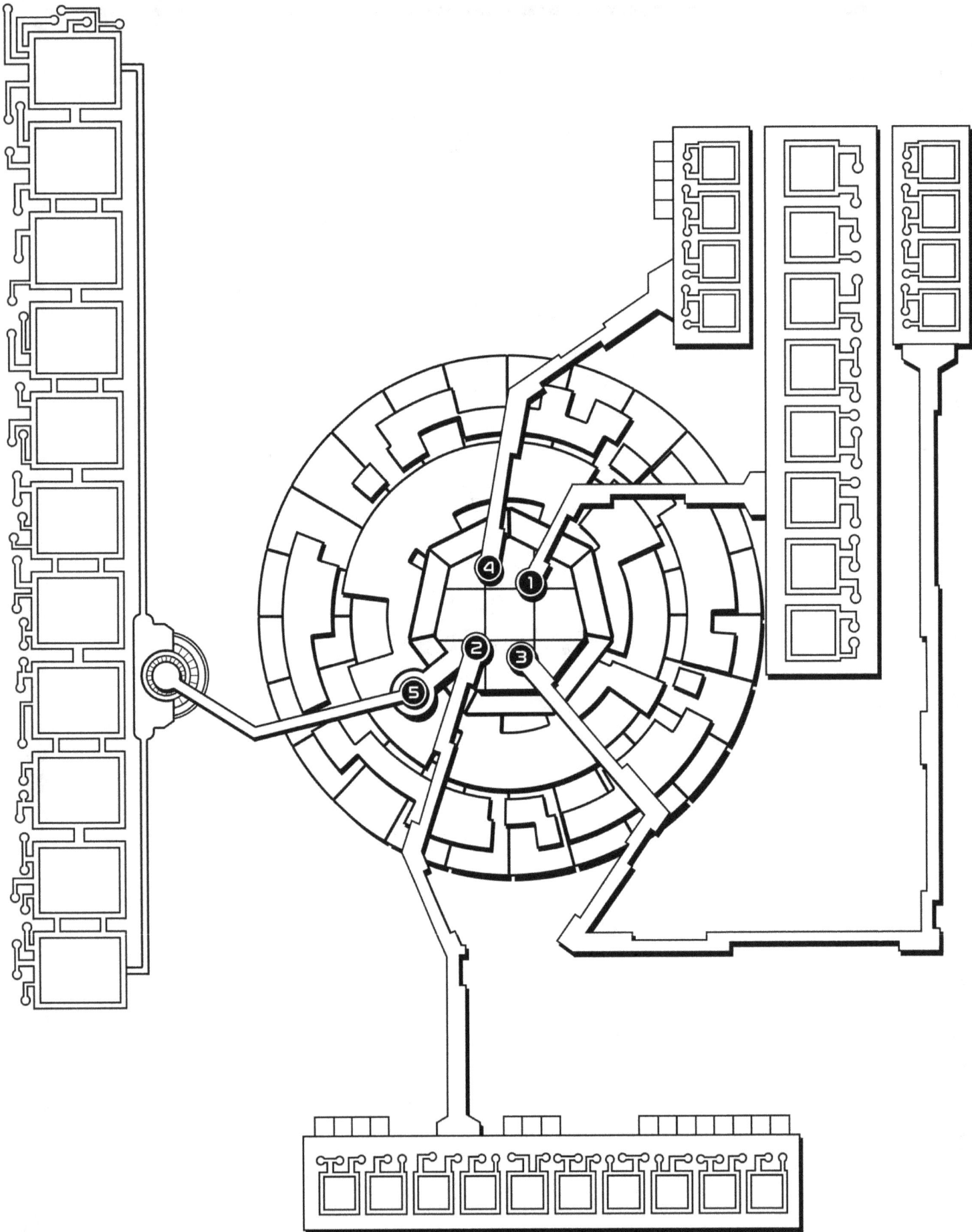

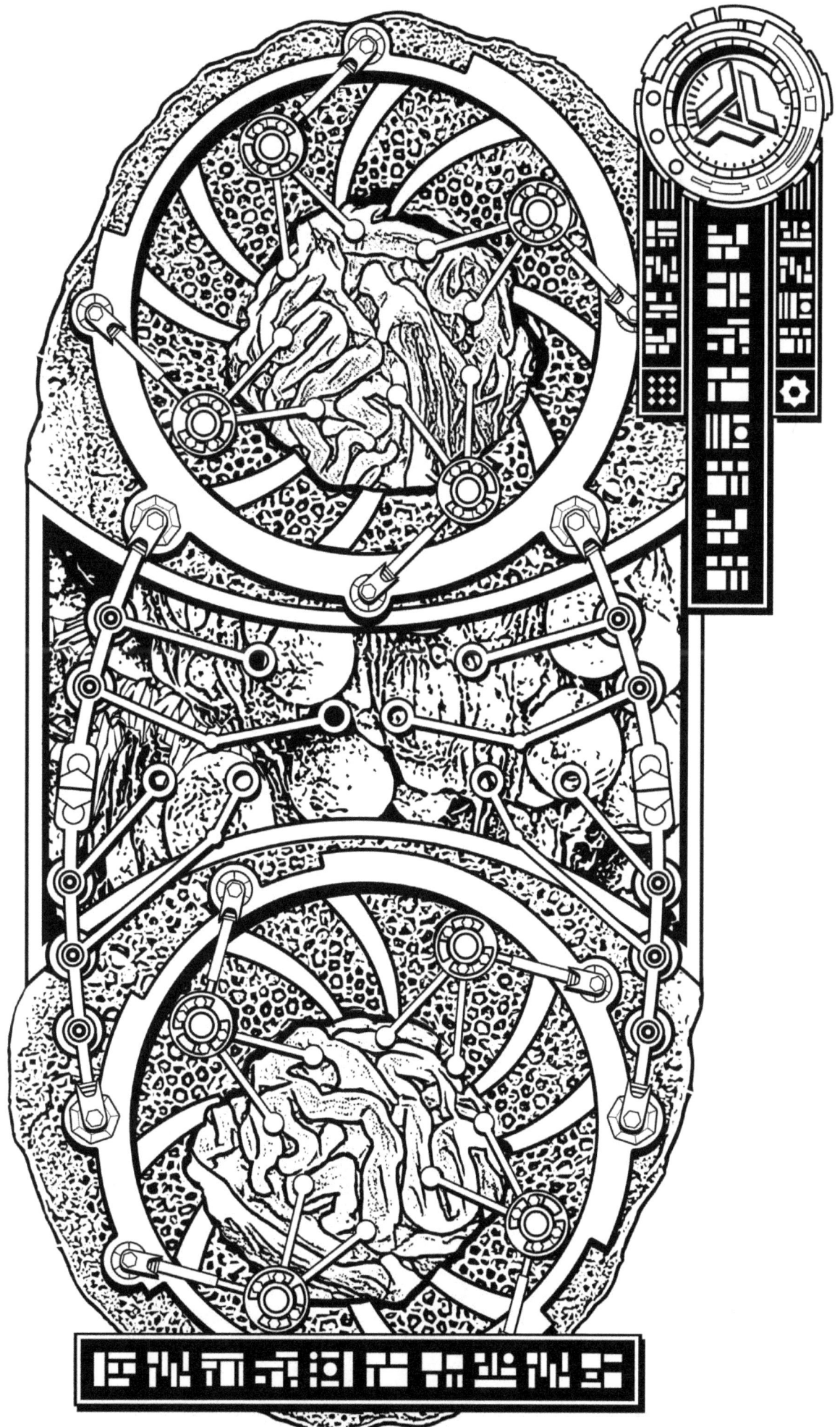

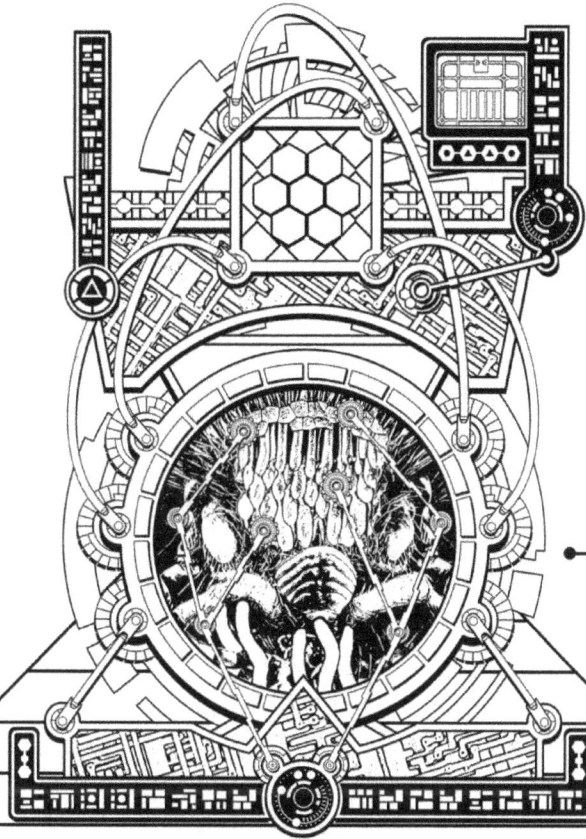

■ CONSTRUCT NAME

1 ——————————— 2 ——————— 3 ———————————

4 ——————— 5 ———————

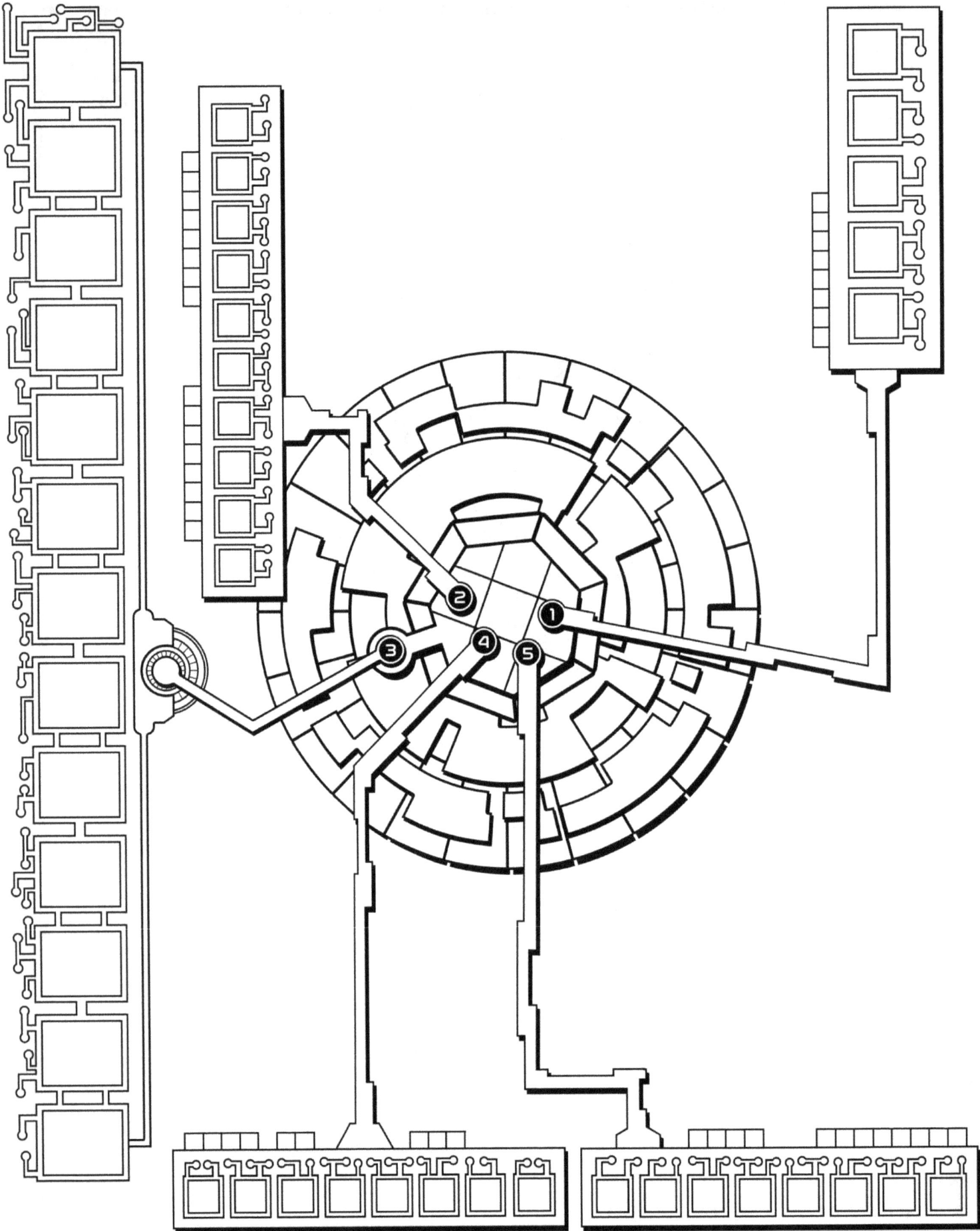

■ DECODE ◀▮▶

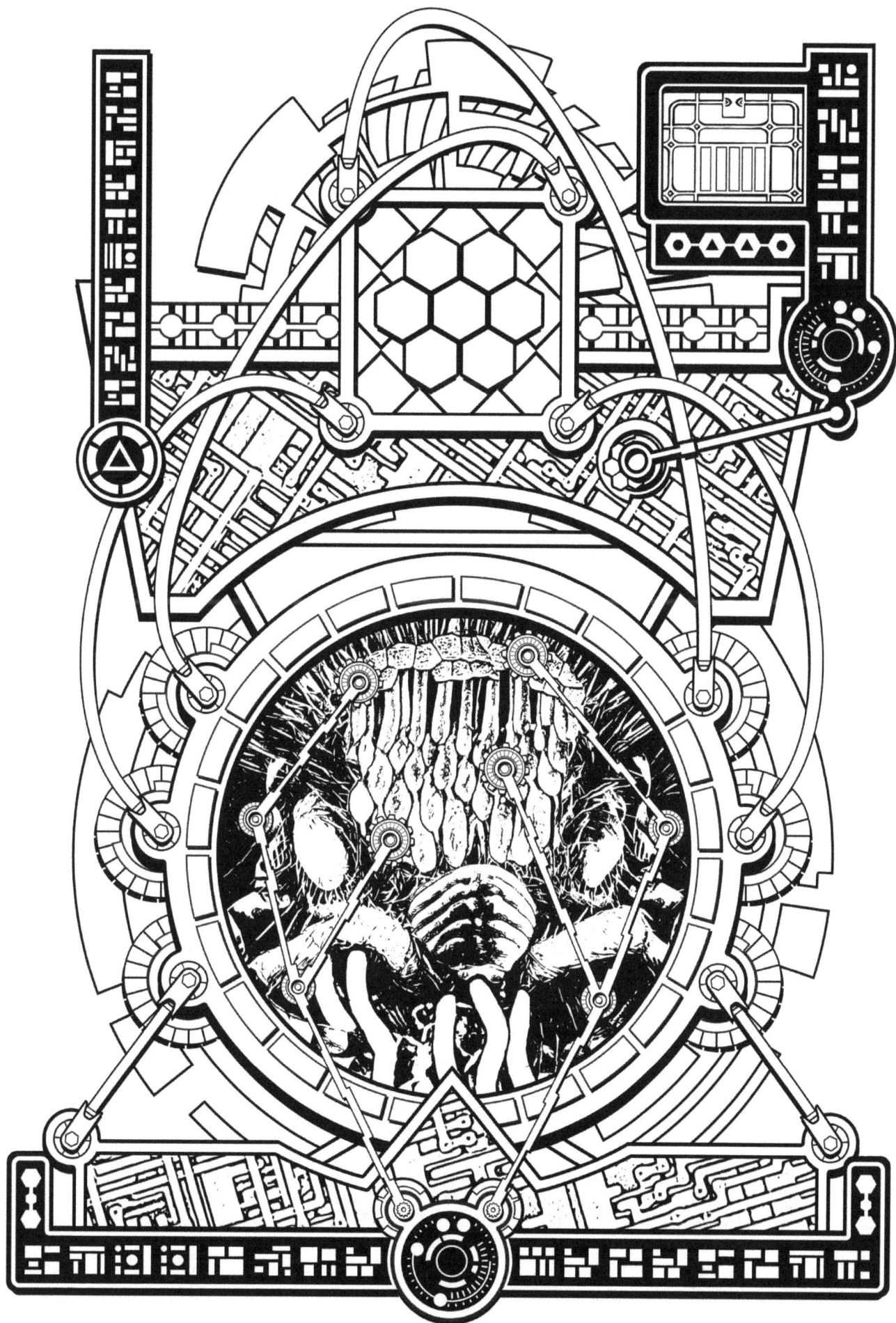

■ CONSTRUCT NAME

1 ——————————— **2** ——————————— **3** ———————————

4 ———————————

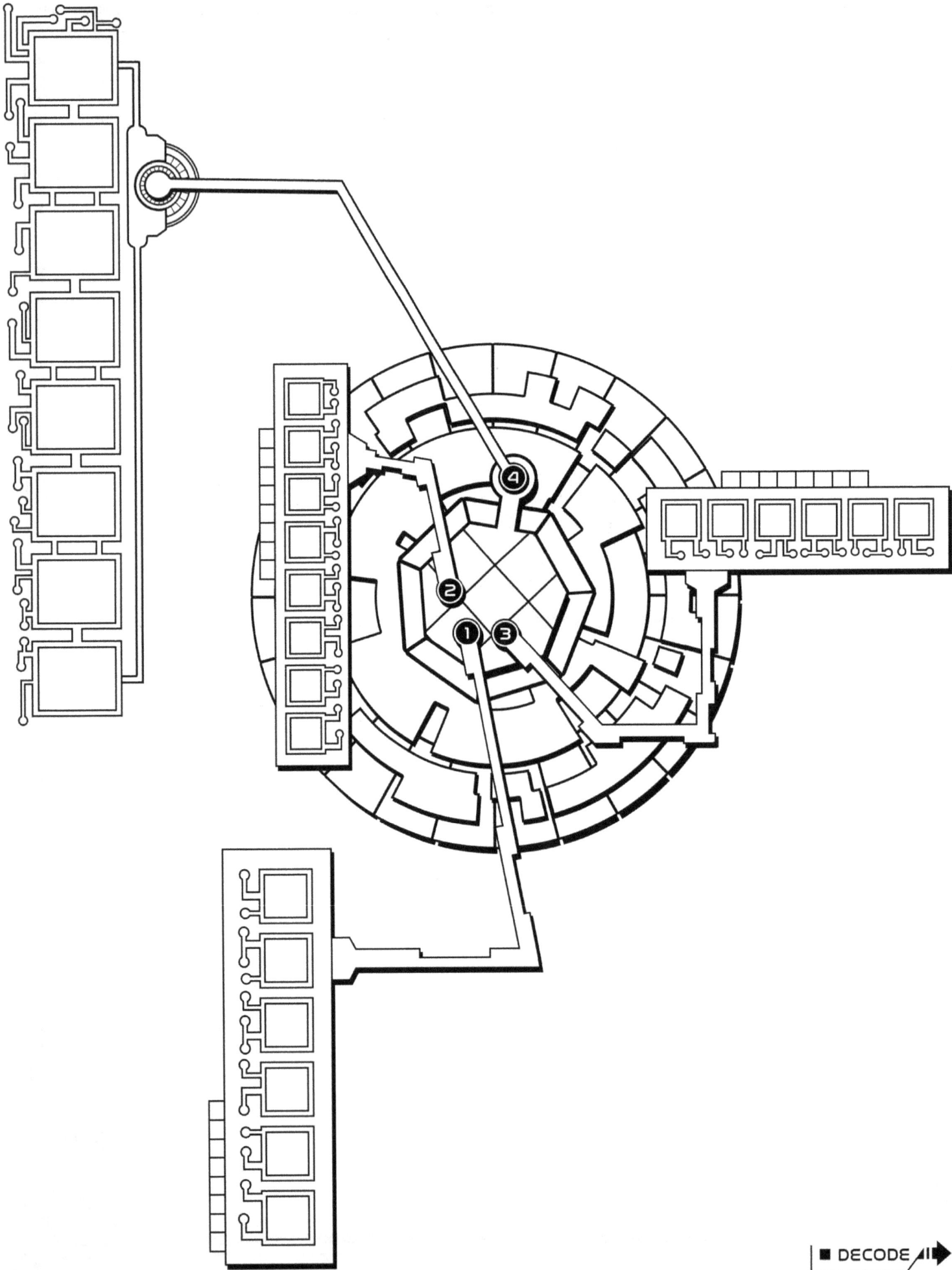

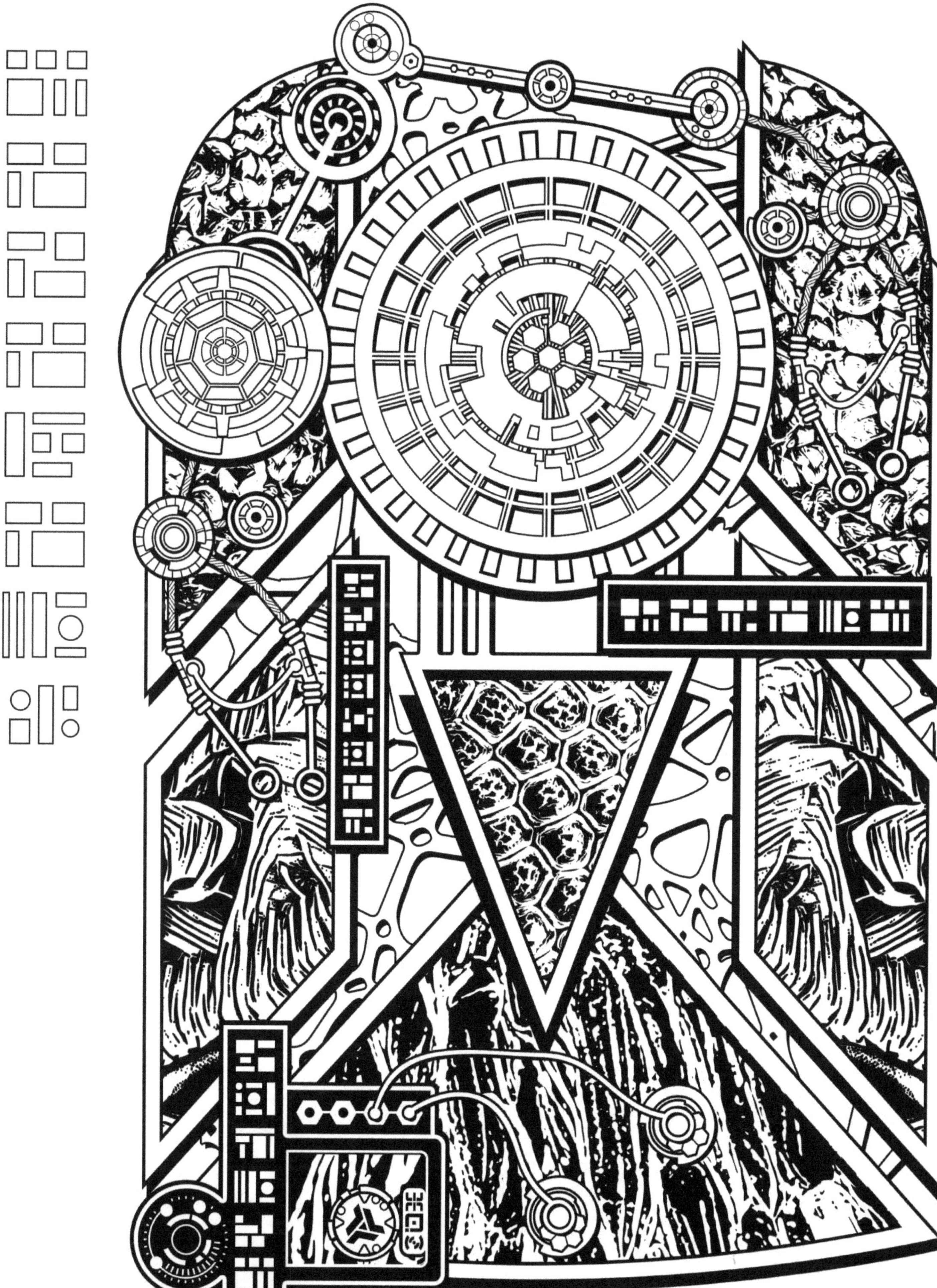

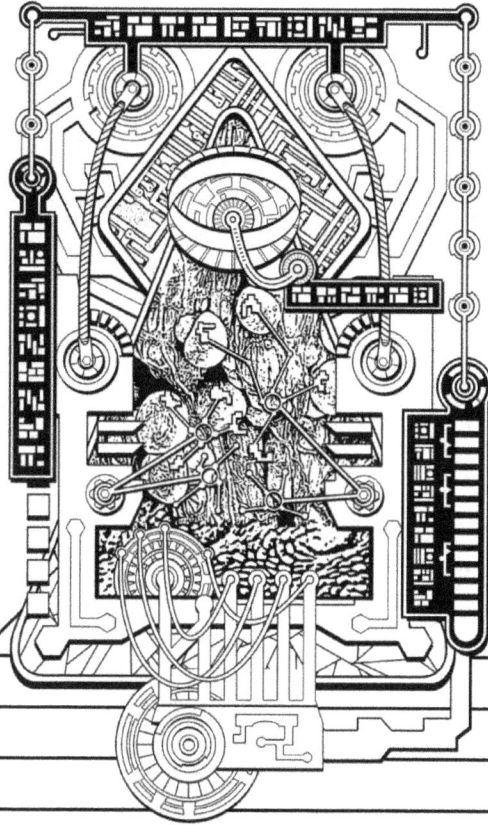

■ CONSTRUCT NAME

1 —————————— 2 —————————— 3 ——————————

4 —————————— 5 ——————————

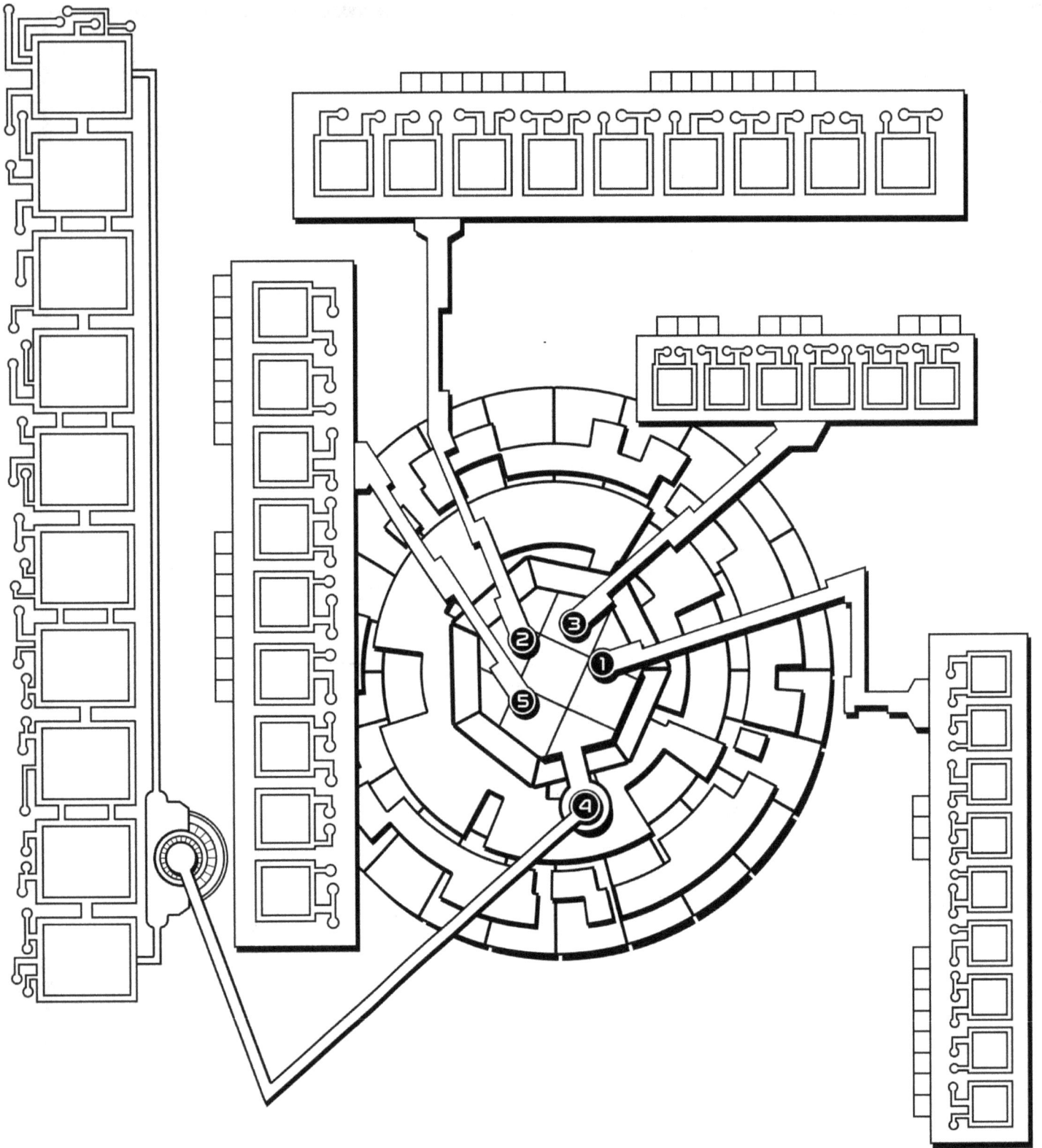

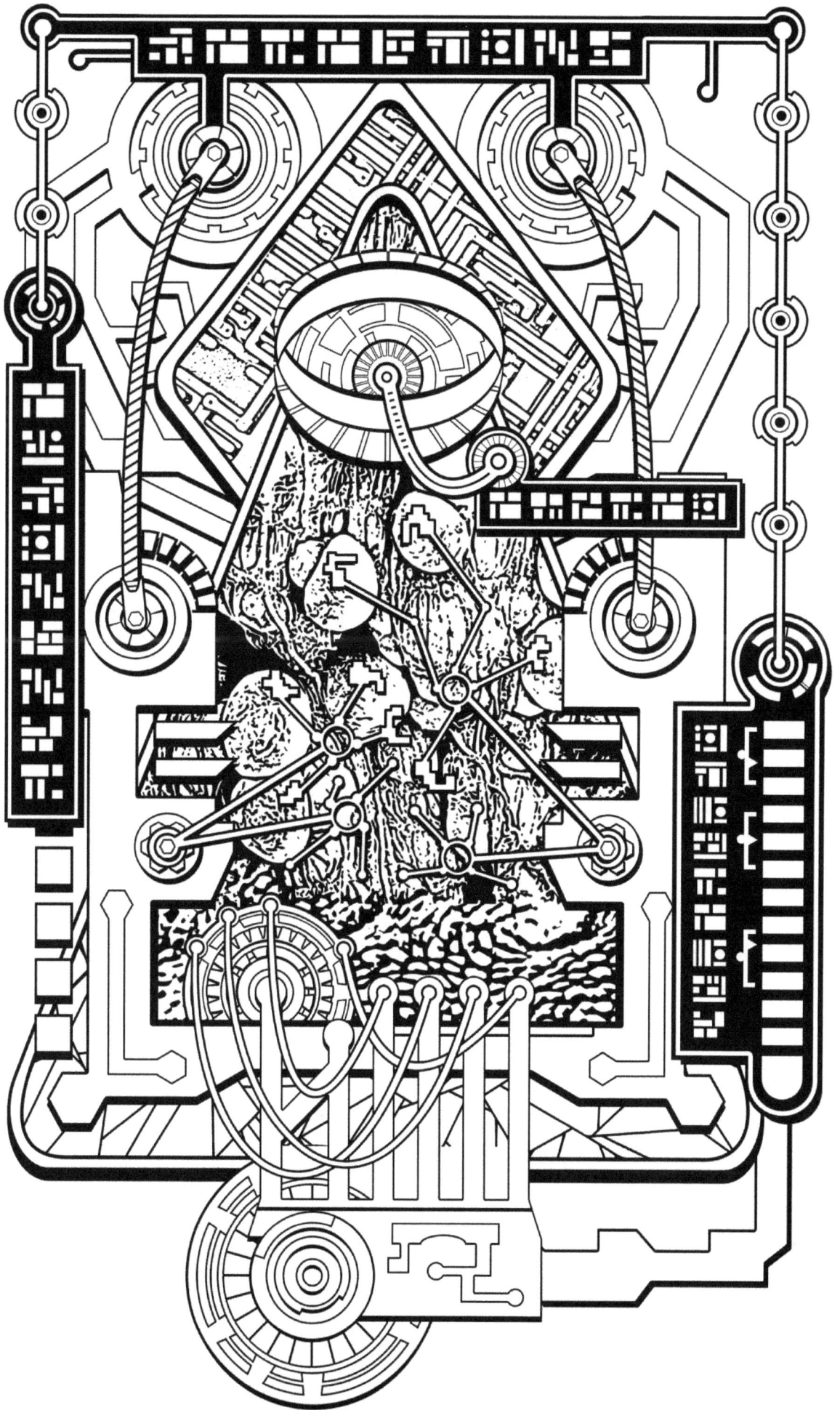

■ CONSTRUCT NAME

① —————————————— ② —————————————— ③ ——————————

④ ——————————————

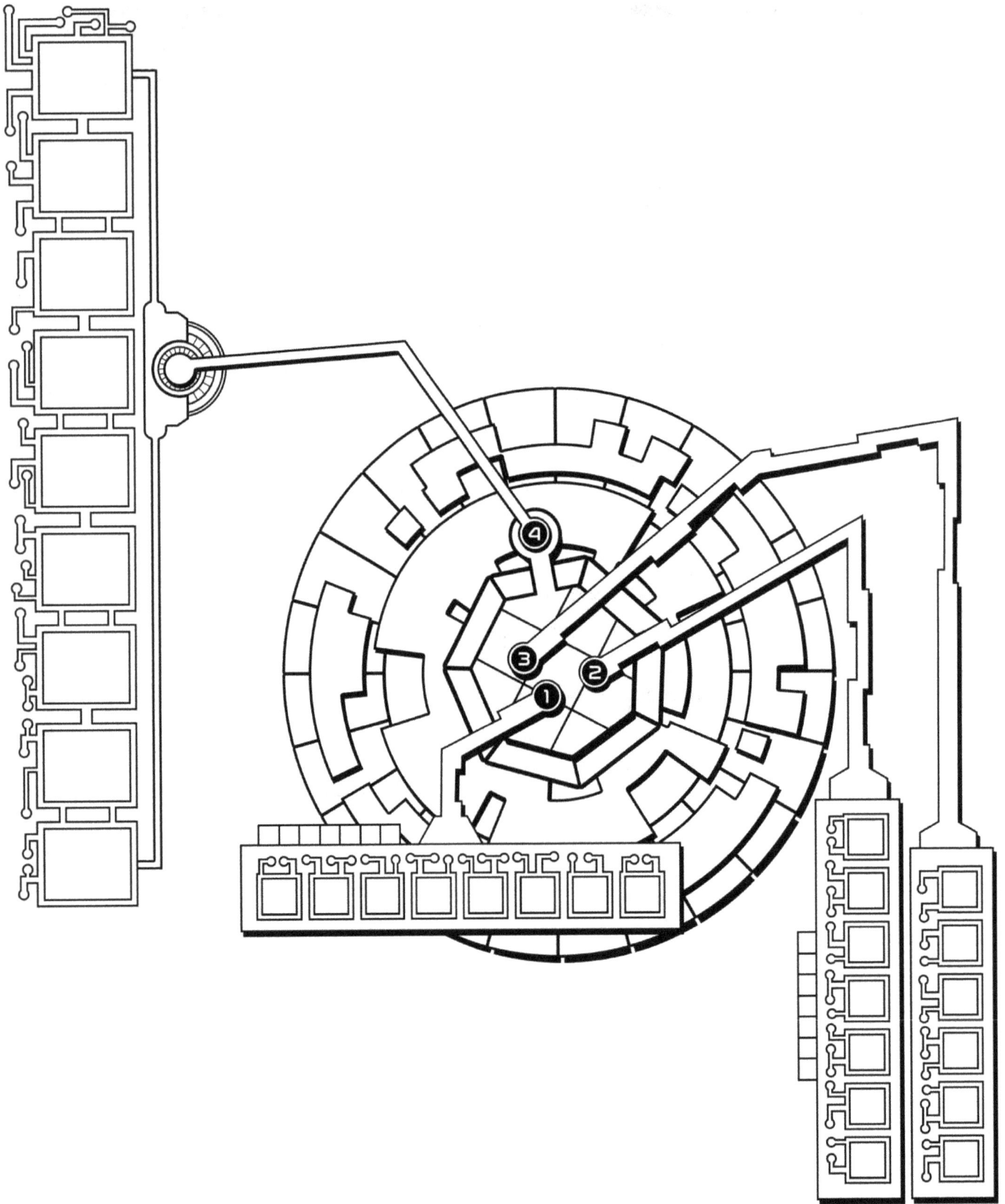

■ CONSTRUCT NAME

① ——————————— ② ——————————— ③ ———————————

④ ———————————

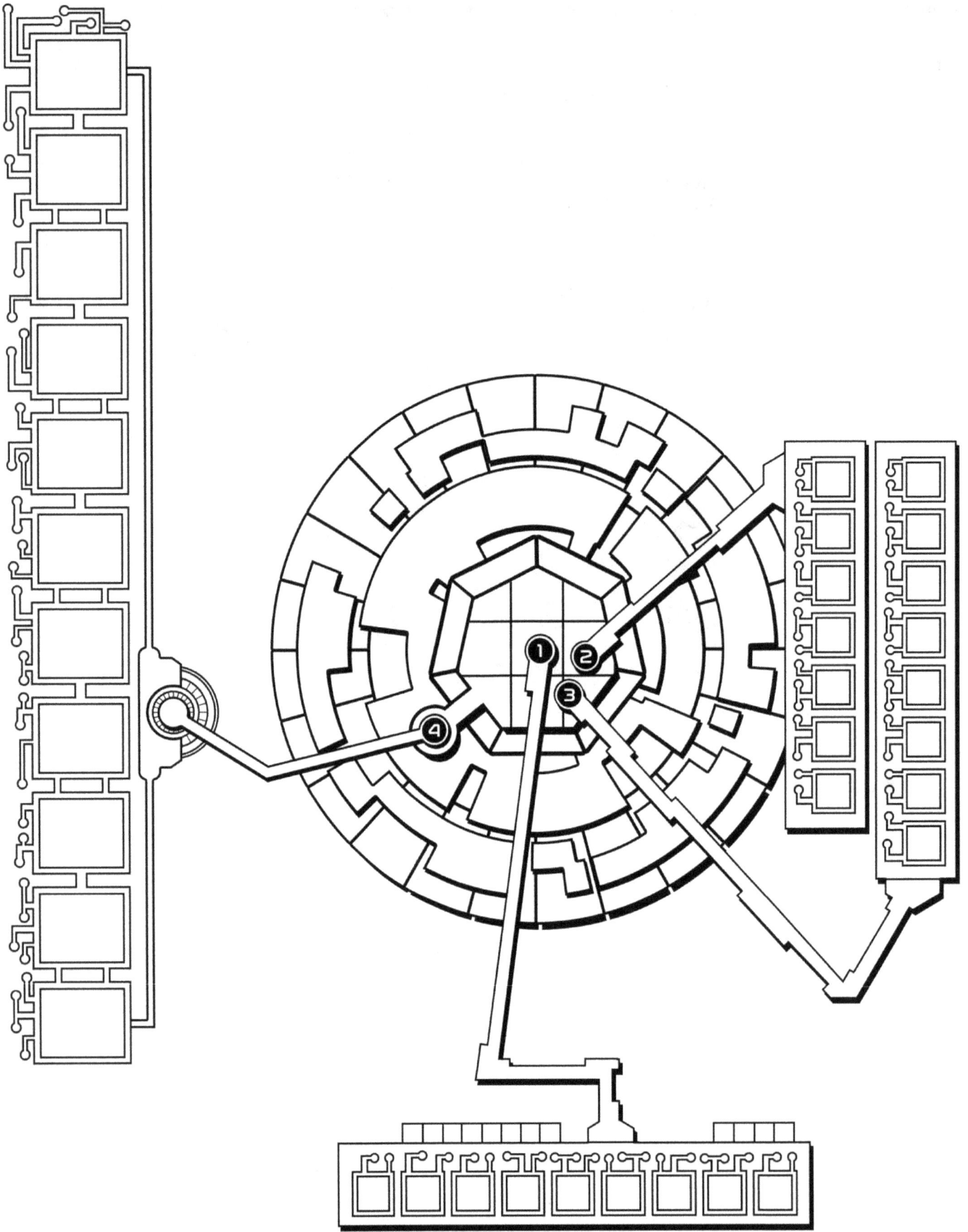

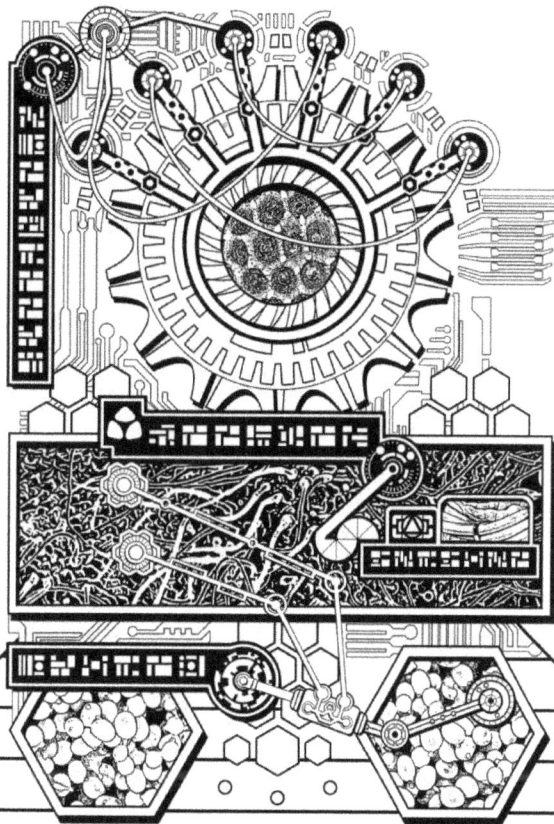

■ CONSTRUCT NAME

① ———————————— ② ———————————— ③ ————————————

④ ———————————— ⑤ ————————————

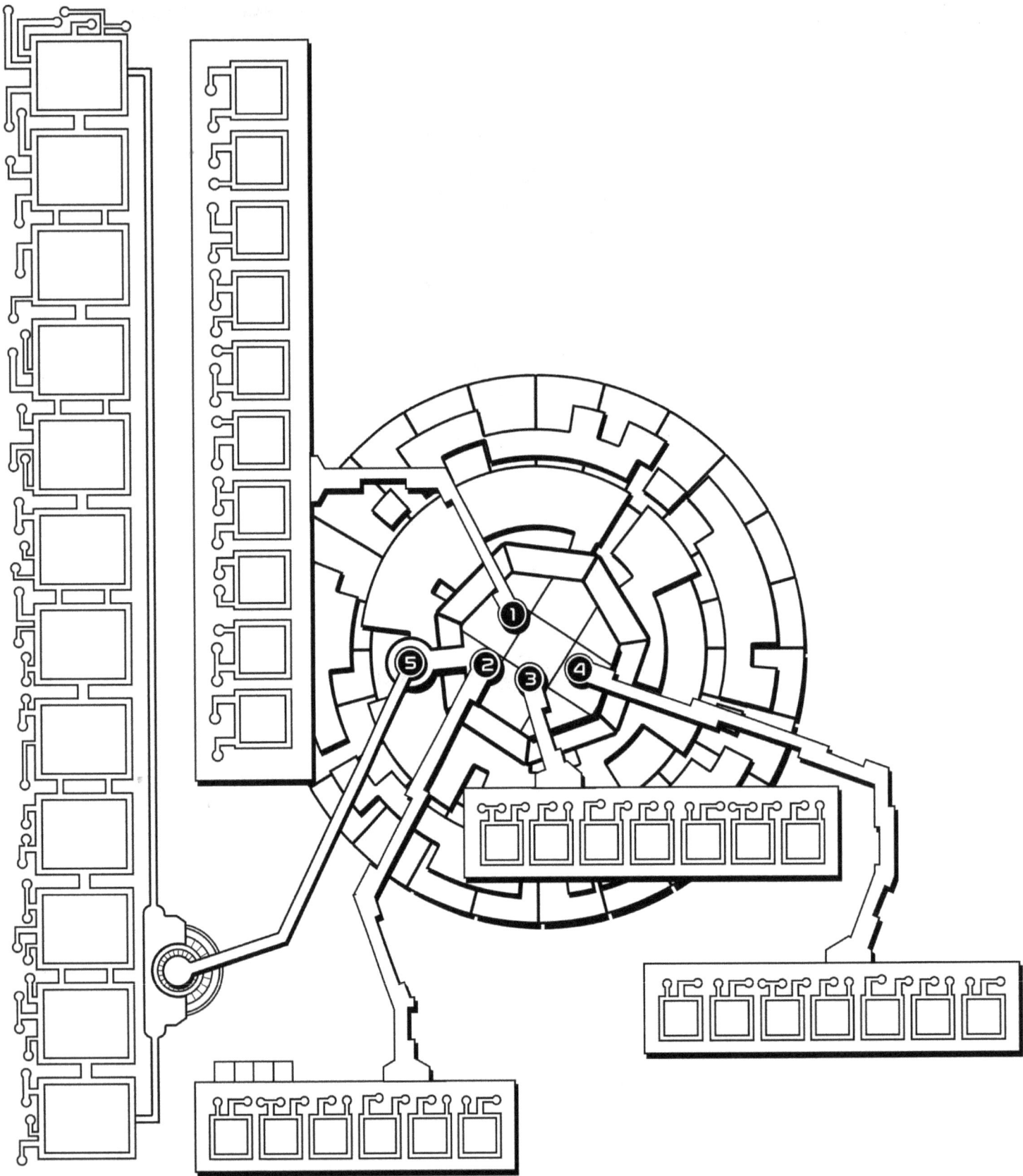

■ CONSTRUCT NAME

① ——————————— ② ——————————— ③ ———————————

④ ——————————— ⑤ ———————————

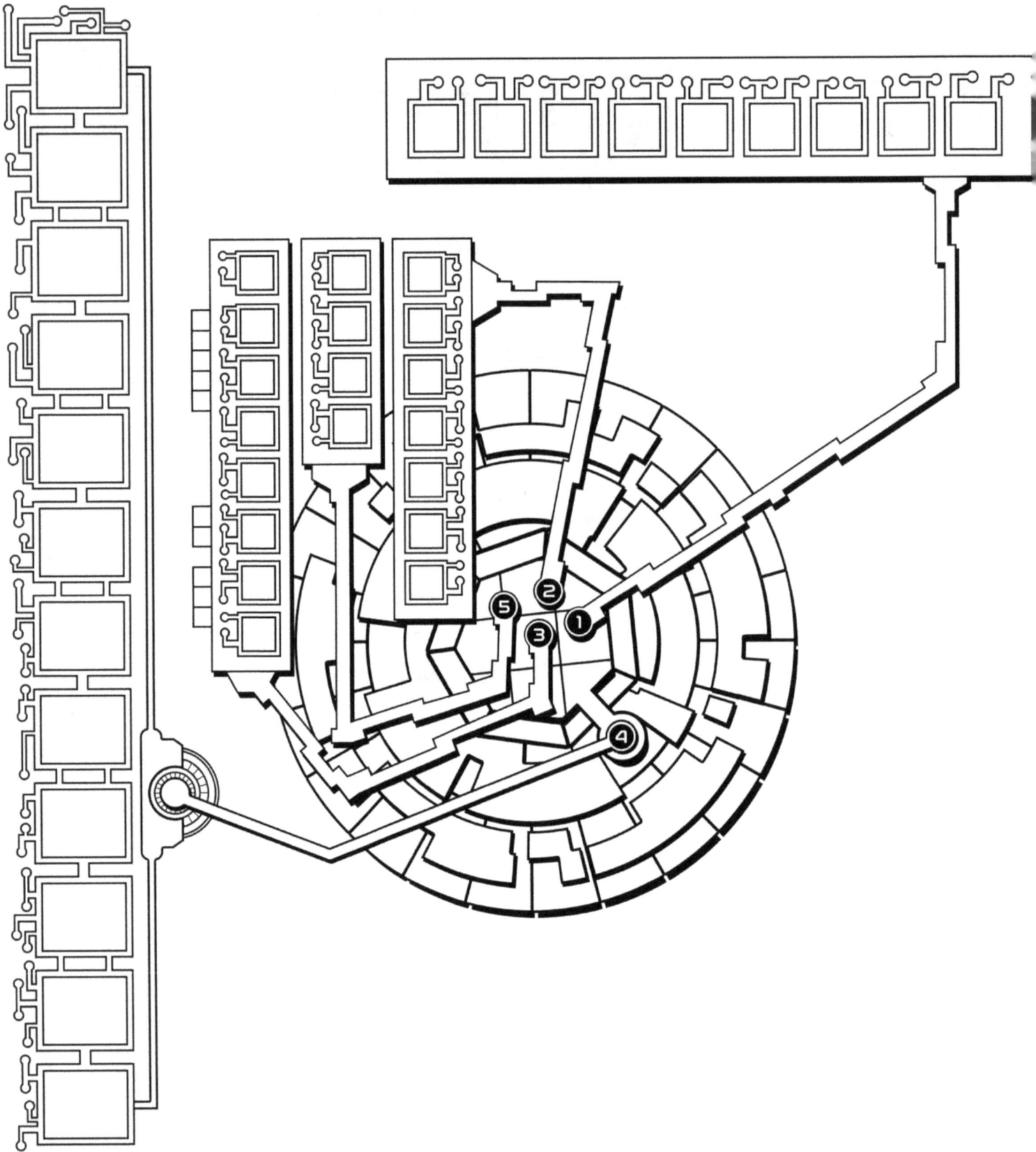

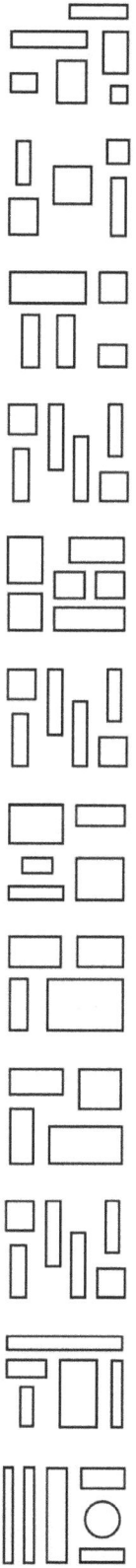

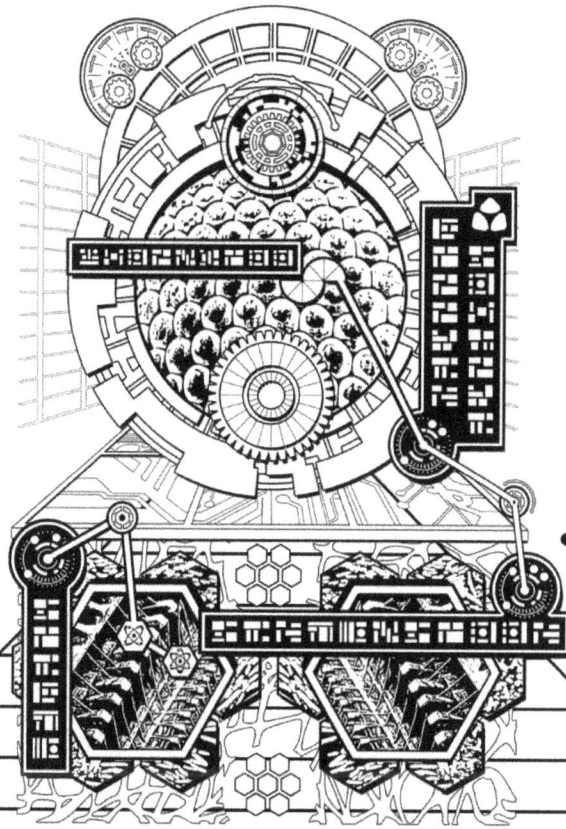

■ CONSTRUCT NAME

1 ———————————— 2 ———————— 3 ————————————

4 ———————————— 5 ———————— 6 ————————————

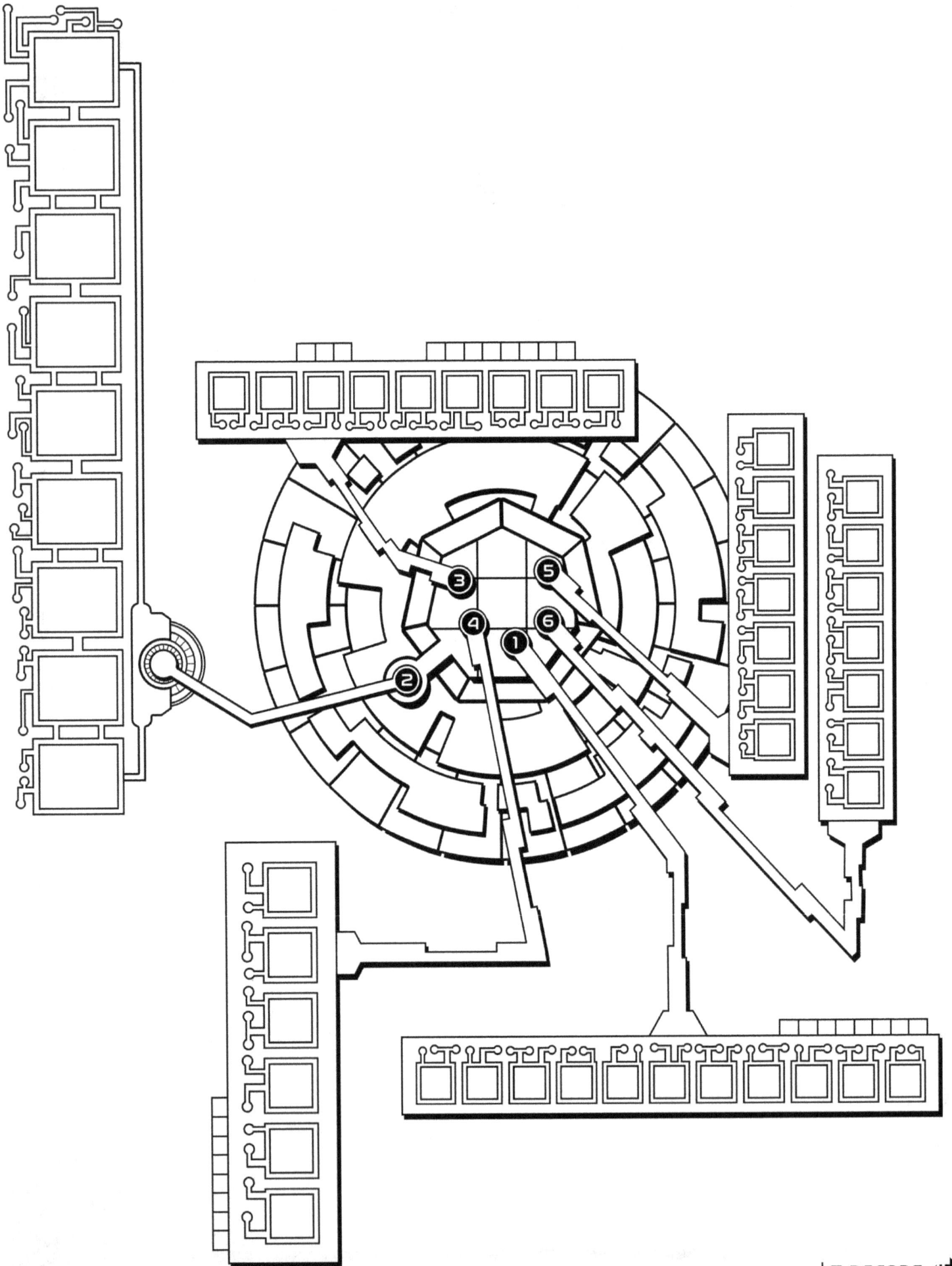

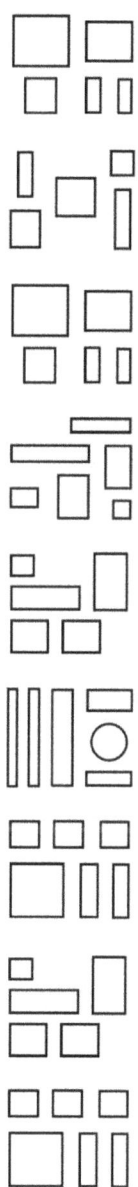

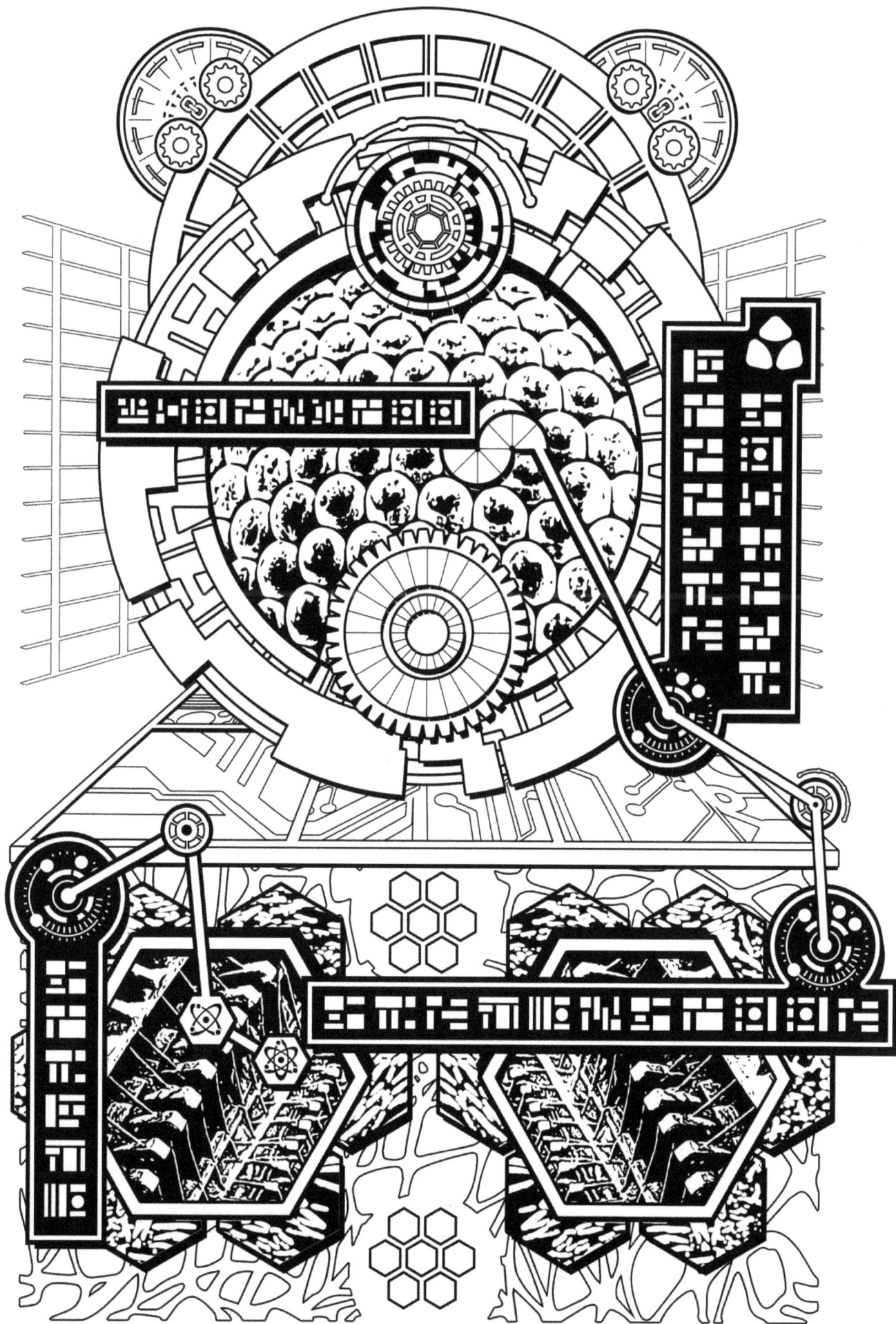

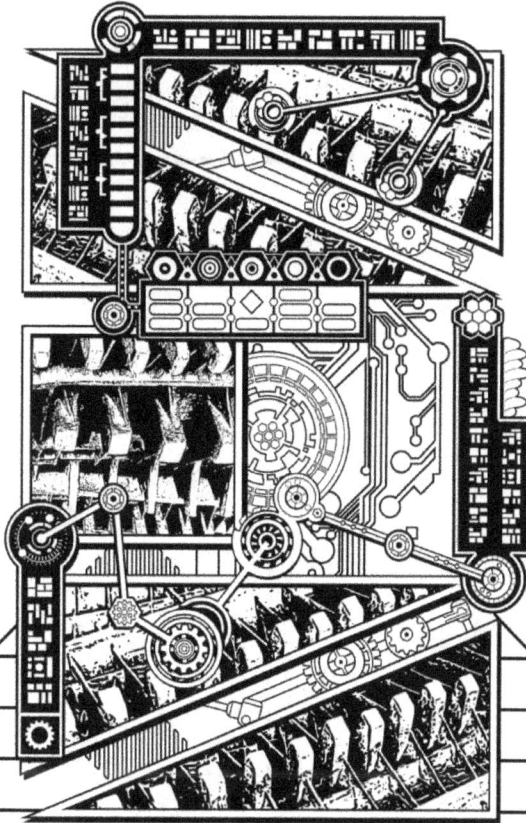

■ CONSTRUCT NAME

1 ───────────────── 2 ───────────────── 3 ─────────────────

4 ───────────────── 5 ───────────────── 6 ─────────────────

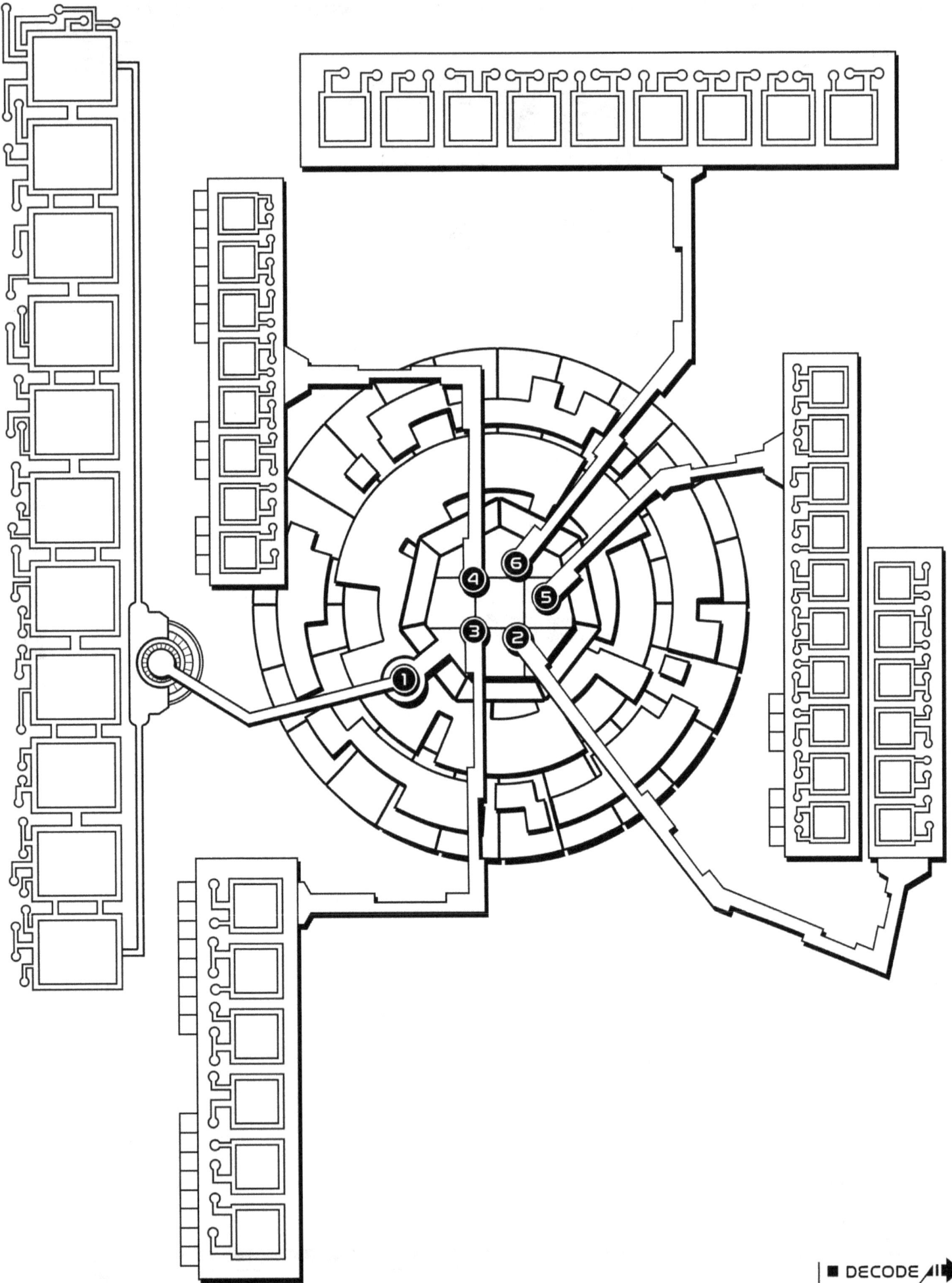

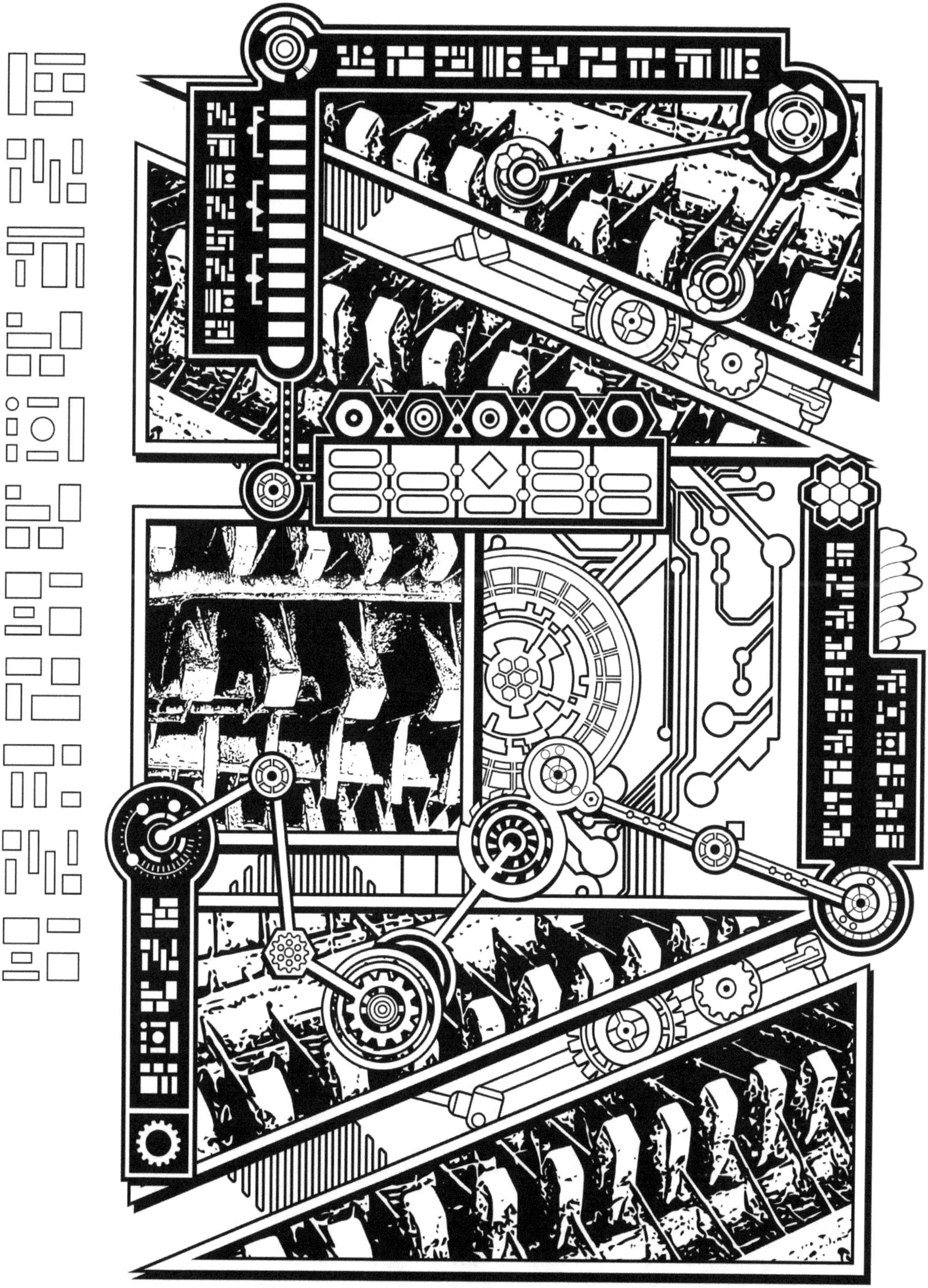

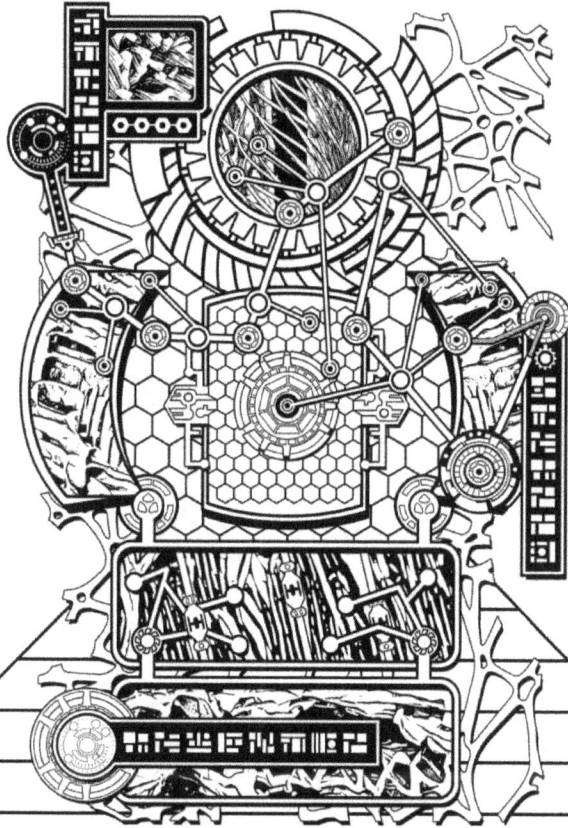

■ CONSTRUCT NAME

① ——————————— ② ——————————— ③ ———————————

④ ———————————

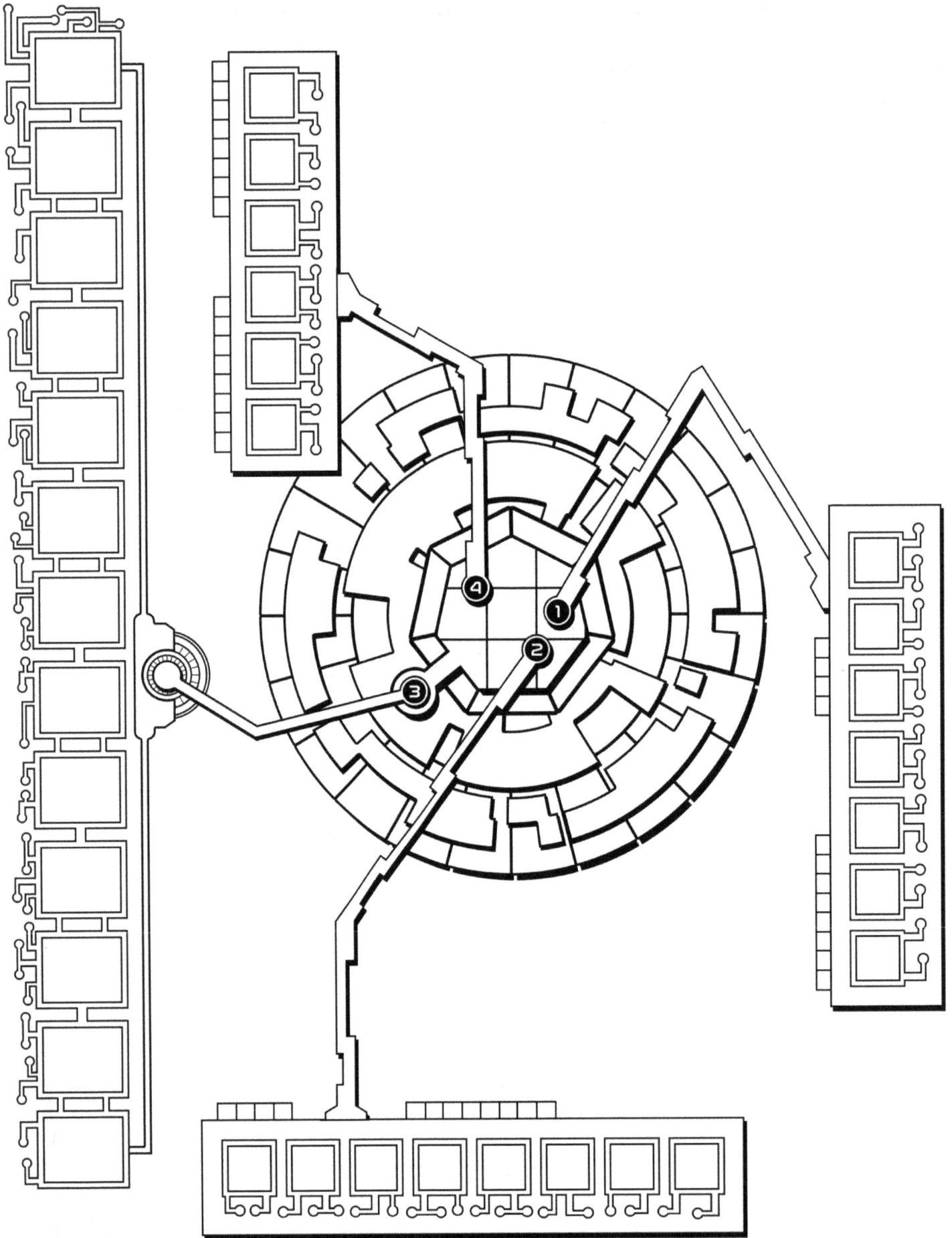

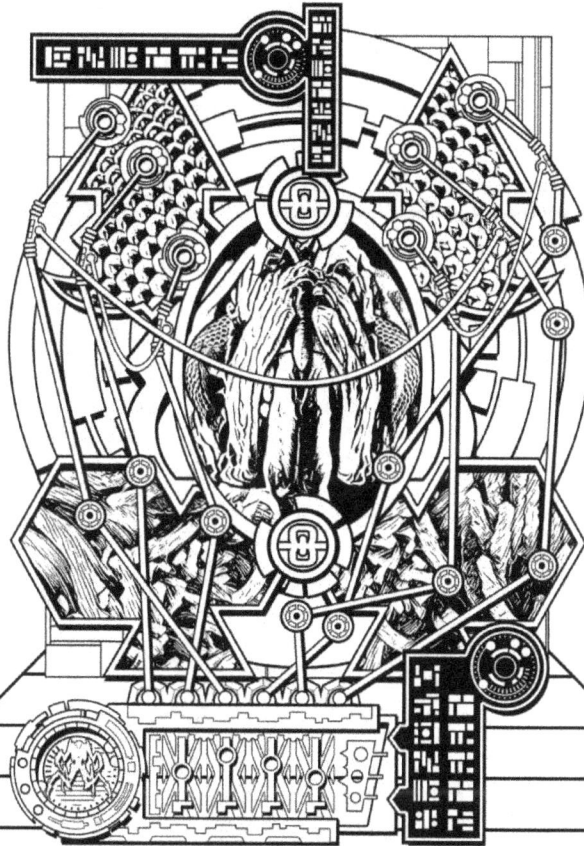

■ CONSTRUCT NAME

① —————————————— ② —————————— ③ ——————————

④ —————————————— ⑤ ——————————

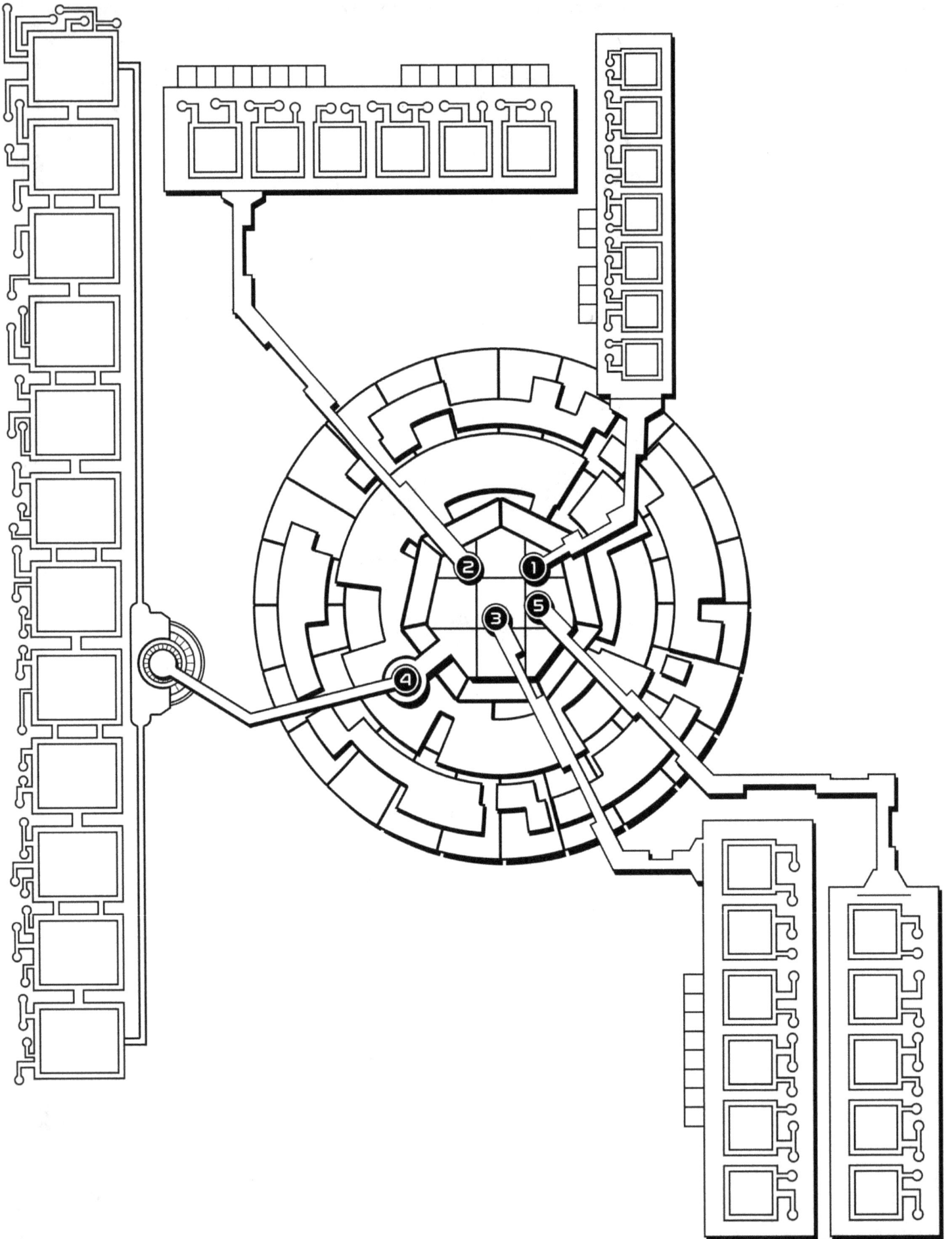

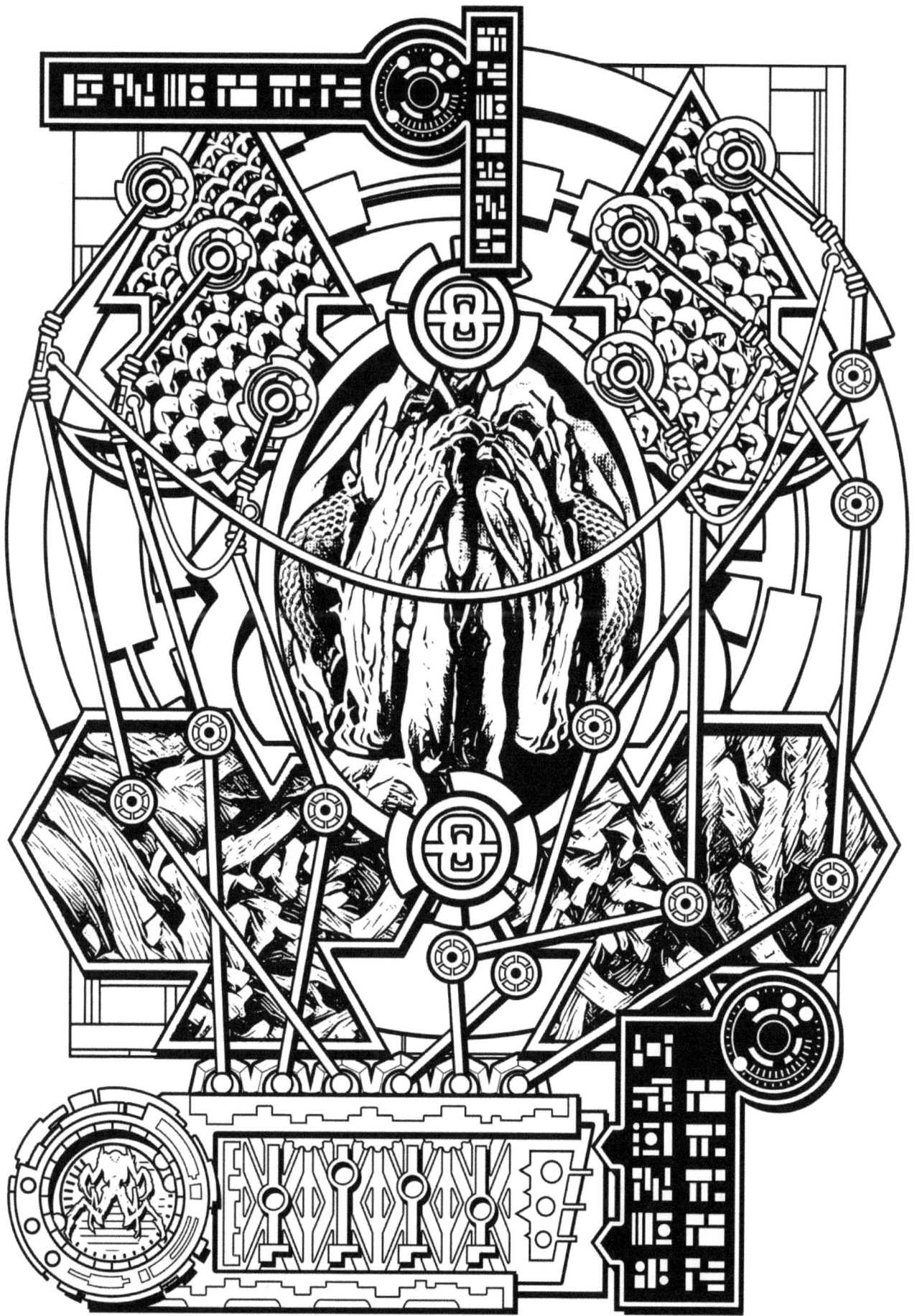

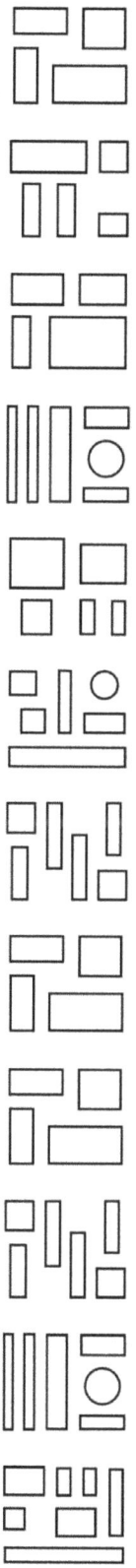

Thank You!

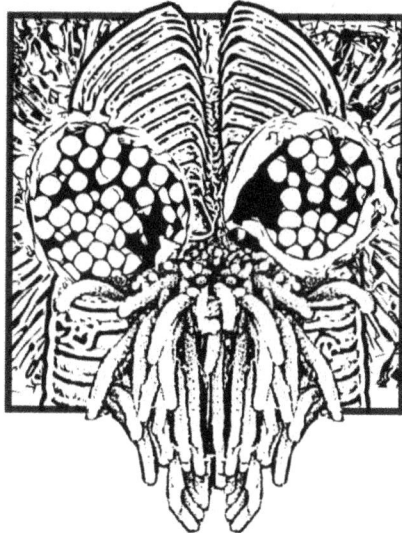

C. Lee Austin is a freelance Digital Art Director who resides in rural Connecticut. He frequently has dreams about UFO's, killer robots, and zombies.

Also, he can not confirm nor deny he owns his very own saucer-shaped spacecraft - so don't ask him about it. Seriously. ☺

Cryptogram Answers

■ Below are the the decoded Construct names in order - <u>upside down</u>.

Z — Dynamic Binary Uplink Transmitting Array

Y — Crystal Symbiont Teleportation Portal

X — Bioelectric Pulsed Field Ionizing Hyperspace Magnetron

W — Cryonically Suspended Multiwall Carbon Battery Cluster

V — Augmented Genetic Material Purification Tank

U — Integrated Neural Pathway Circuit Architecture

T — Xenogenic Protein Enriched Biocomputer

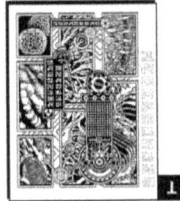

S — Harmonic Thermal Matrix Inhibitor

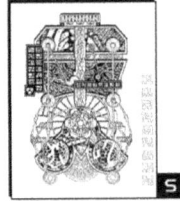

R — Longrange Parabolic Astral Projection Amplifier

Q — Cloned Cellular Strand Databank

P — Micro Cybernetic Gravitational Collapse Detector

O — Expanded Bioplasmic Hive Mind Intensifier

N — Cyclonic Quartz Stream Subspace Generator

M — Powercore Protective Membrane

L — Prehensile Gestalt Intelligent Active Neural Plasma Bridge

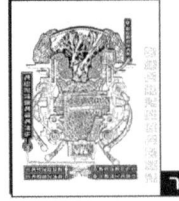

K — Biological Substance Accumulation Canisters

J — Mutation Targeting Polymorphic Nanohunter

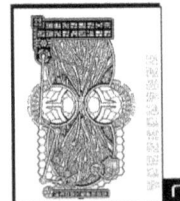

I — Biogenic Elevated Differencing Engine

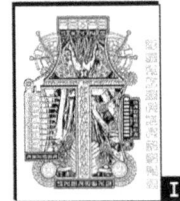

H — Bacterial Protoplasm Nanotube Incubation Chamber

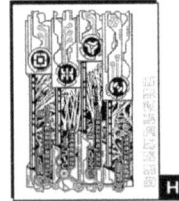

G — Remote Control Robotic Ganglion Capsules

F — Biotic Enhanced Extrasensory Perception Analyzer

E — Antimatter Activated Event Horizon Gravity Anchor

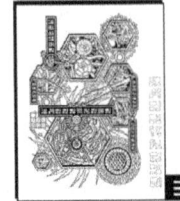

D — Hyperdrive Navigation Fiber Optic Biochips

C — Fortified Mnemonic Mind Siphon

B — Biomimetic Fibrous Silica Membranes

A — Nanofluidic Synthetic Sensory Antenna

www.ingramcontent.com/pod-product-compliance
Lightning Source LLC
Chambersburg PA
CBHW081148040426
42445CB00015B/1805